ROMEO & JULIET

ROMEO & JULIET

William Shakespeare

Series Editor: Jane Bachman

Consulting Editor: Skip Nicholson

NTC Publishing Group
Lincolnwood, Illinois USA

Cover illustration: From the Art Collection of the Folger Shakespeare Library

Interior illustrations: Diane Novario

1997 Printing

Manufactured in the United States of America.
Library of Congress Catalog Card Number: 92-60870

7 8 9 0 VP 9 8 7 6 5 4

CONTENTS

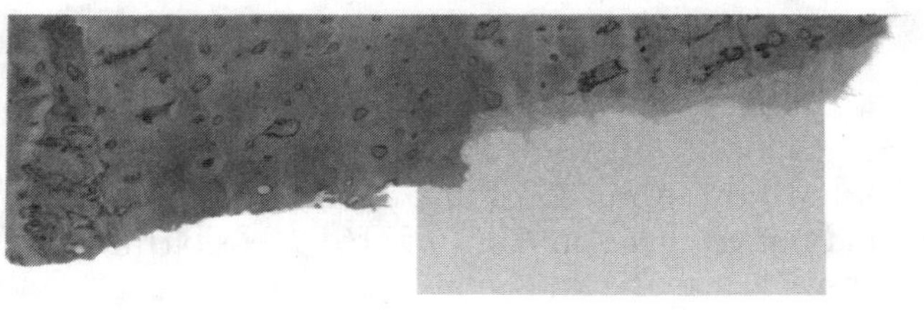

Introducing Shakespeare

Most of what we know about William Shakespeare's life is based only on public records or on allusions to his work in various letters and diaries of his day. He was baptized on April 26, 1564, in Trinity Church in Stratford-upon-Avon and buried there on April 25, 1616. His birthday is usually celebrated on April 23, also the date of his death.

Stratford is in Warwickshire, a county northwest of London. In Shakespeare's time it was a small market town. His father, John Shakespeare, was a prosperous townsman who made gloves and was also a tanner as well as a dealer in farm produce. John Shakespeare held various town offices. However, in 1586 he was forced into bankruptcy because he could not pay his debts. Mary Arden, Shakespeare's mother, was the daughter of Robert Arden, a well-to-do farmer who left her money and a small estate in addition to several properties he had given her before his death. For most of their life together, the parents of William Shakespeare were reasonably well off.

William Shakespeare was the third of eight children, two of whom died before his birth and one of whom died when William was a boy. Only a sister, Joan, survived him; one of his brothers, Edmund, may have been an actor.

Shakespeare probably attended the grammar school in Stratford, where he might have learned Latin and Greek. Records show that he married Anne Hathaway, eight years his senior, in Stratford in 1582. He and Anne had three children: Susanna, born in 1583, and twins Judith and Hamnet, born in 1585. Hamnet died at the age of eleven.

The next record of Shakespeare is in 1592, when he was evidently in London. In the pamphlet *A Groatsworth of Wit*, addressed to fellow playwrights who were university graduates (as Shakespeare was not), Robert Greene bitterly refers to Shakespeare as "an upstart crow, beautified with our feathers, that with his Tyger's hart wrapt in a Player's hyde supposes he is as well able to bombast out a blanke verse as the best of you; and being an absolute *Johannes fac totum*, is in his owne conceit the only Shake-scene in a country." The phrase "Tyger's hart" refers to a line in *Henry VI, Part 3* by Shakespeare, a play probably first produced in 1591. *Johannes fac totum* means "jack-of-all-trades." Some scholars think that Shakespeare began his career as an actor, probably sometime before 1592, and that when he began to write plays, he angered many established playwrights, such as Greene.

Although the date of Shakespeare's arrival in London is not certain, it is known that some of his early plays were produced by an acting company known as Lord Pembroke's Men. He might have acted with this company as well. In 1594 he became a member of a company called Lord

Chamberlain's Men, for which he wrote many successful plays, and in 1599 he became a partner in the newly constructed Globe Theatre. This partnership assured his financial success and enabled him to invest in considerable property, both in Stratford and in London.

Shakespeare early achieved recognition as a poet, and in 1598 one writer referred to him as "mellifluous and honey-tongued" when writing of Shakespeare's long poem *Venus and Adonis,* first published in 1593. All in all, some 37 plays and 154 sonnets are attributed to Shakespeare.

Critics sometimes divide his dramatic career into four periods: the Early Period (1564–1594); the Period of Comedies and Histories (1595–1601); the Period of Tragedies (1602–1608); and the Period of Romances (1609–1616). The first attempt at publishing a collection of his plays was in 1623, when the First Folio was published. (The printer's term *folio* refers to the folding of the printed sheets.) The First Folio contains thirty-six plays. A later play, *Pericles,* was added to the second edition of the Third Folio in 1664. During his life, however, eighteen of Shakespeare's plays were published in quarto editions. (Again a printer's term, a *quarto* was a smaller, squarer book than a folio.)

In 1611 or 1612 Shakespeare returned permanently to Stratford where he wrote his last plays. The cause of Shakespeare's death at age fifty-two is unknown. His wife and both daughters survived him and are mentioned in his will, which also mentions small bequests to various friends and to the poor of Stratford.

Introducing *Romeo and Juliet*

Romeo and Juliet is one of Shakespeare's most popular plays and very often the first Shakespearian play read by students in school. It is a love story, but as the play's Prologue states, the lovers are "star-crossed" and destined to die. That the reader and audience know the outcome of the story before the play begins in no way diminishes the play's appeal, however.

Shakespeare's main source for his play was a long poem by Englishman Arthur Brooke called *The Tragicall Historye of Romeo and Juliet* (1562), but the origins of the story are much older. A fifth-century Greek story tells of a woman who swallowed a sleep-inducing potion to avoid an unwanted marriage. In a fifteenth-century Italian collection of short works appears the story of Mariotto of Siena and Gianozza who fall in love and are married by a friar. When Mariotto kills a man, he must flee. To prevent her marriage to someone else, Gianozza takes a sleeping medicine, is entombed, and then rescued. Mariotto learns of her death before receiving a letter from the friar telling him of the deception. He returns to look for his wife, but she has gone in search of him. Mariotto is arrested and put to death and Gianozza dies in a convent.

In a later version, also published in Italy, the lovers are Romeo and Giuletta, the setting is Verona, and the story takes place against the backdrop of two feuding families, the Montecchi and the Capelli. In 1554 Matteo Bandello, an Italian writer, included the tale in his *Novelle*, which was then translated into French in 1559. Brooke apparently based his poem on the French translation. There is no definite indication that Shakespeare read any version of the story except that of Brooke. Shakespeare expanded and changed the roles of several characters present in Brooke's version and compressed the action into a few days instead of the nine months over which events happen in Brooke's poem.

Shakespeare probably wrote the play in 1595, making it one of his earliest works. It was first published in what is known as a bad quarto in 1597. *Quarto* is a printer's term that refers to the size of a folded sheet. The term *bad* means that the play was not printed from Shakespeare's manuscript but probably set down from the play as memorized by one or more actors. A second quarto, published in 1599, is considered to be more accurate and is the basis for later editions of the play.

Although *Romeo and Juliet* is a tragedy, it has much in common with Shakespeare's comedies. Both Mercutio and the Nurse seem to belong more to comedy than to tragedy, and the theme of romantic love is common to the comedies. However, we are constantly reminded throughout the play of the ancient feud between the Montagues and Capulets, the unreasoning family hatred that helps bring about the lovers' tragic fate.

A Note on Shakespeare's Language

A writer can communicate feelings and appeal to your senses only through words. Shakespeare achieves many of his most dramatic effects in *Romeo and Juliet* by using powerful imagery. In Act I, Scene 1, when Montague's wife asks Benvolio whether he has seen Romeo, Benvolio replies that he saw him "an hour before . . . sun peered forth the golden window of the east," an image that immediately brings to mind the beginnings of dawn.

In Act I, Scene 4, Mercutio creates a miniature world when he describes Queen Mab, whose chariot is an empty hazelnut. In Act II, Scene 2, when Romeo spies Juliet at her window, he wishes that he were a glove upon her hand "that I might touch that cheek." And later he says "How silver-sweet sound lovers' tongues . . . like softest music."

Critic Caroline Spurgeon has written of the many images of light in the play. Look for these as well as other recurring images as you read, for they will help you understand the emotions expressed and the themes of the play.

Introducing the Globe Theatre

The Globe is the sixteenth-century theatre most closely associated with Shakespeare, for he had a financial interest in it, acted there, and wrote many of his plays for the actors at the Globe.

James Burbage built the first theatre in London, known simply as the Theatre, in 1576. In 1599 the Theatre was dismantled by Burbage's two sons, Richard and Cuthbert, and rebuilt as the Globe on the opposite side of the Thames River. Richard and Cuthbert Burbage held a half interest in the Globe, and five actors divided the other half interest, among them Shakespeare.

The Globe burned in 1613 when, during a performance of Shakespeare's *Henry VIII*, a cannon discharged backstage and touched off a fire in the thatched roof. The Globe was rebuilt on the same site, and we know something about its features from the surviving specifications for another theatre.

In 1600 Philip Henslowe built the Fortune theatre, and the contractor was directed to build the Fortune like the Globe, with at least one exception: it was to be square instead of polygonal.

There are a few other clues about the appearance of the Globe. Several period drawings and engravings of London and of theatres, including the Globe, still exist. Perhaps the most interesting recent event was the 1989 discovery and excavation of the remains of the Rose Theatre, built in London in 1586 quite near the Globe.

Suppose for a moment that you are a playgoer. It is early afternoon and you have reached the Globe on foot, or you have been rowed in a ferry across the Thames from the north side. As you approach the theatre, you see a flag flying from the top to indicate that a performance will be given today. Since the theatre holds 2,000 to 3,000 people, and most Londoners are avid playgoers, you soon find yourself in the midst of a huge throng.

When you enter the theatre, you can look up at the sky, for the circular area, or pit, in front of the stage is not roofed. Turning, you note that there are three levels of spectator's galleries on three sides of the theatre and a gallery above and at the back of the stage as well.

The floor of the theatre is about 5 ½ feet below the stage and about 70 feet in diameter. If you have only a penny to spend, this is where you will stand, elbow to elbow with other spectators, to see the performance. If you can afford more, you will ascend the stairs to one of the galleries, where you will be able to sit protected from the weather.

The stage itself is a little over forty feet wide and about twenty-seven feet deep. You have heard that the floor of the stage contains a trap door, a convenient opening for the emergence of special effects such as smoke.

At the back of the stage are two (possibly three) doors, which open inward and may be covered by curtains. The actors will appear through these doors from the tiring house, or dressing rooms, behind the stage. The central area behind the curtains may be used as a small "discovery space" for some plays. In a performance of *Hamlet*, for example, Polonius hides behind the curtain before he is stabbed.

If the gallery above and at the back of the stage is needed for the performance, there will be no spectators there. In *Romeo and Juliet*, this area represents Juliet's window, where she stands to speak to Romeo below.

The roof above the stage is decorated and is supported by at least two pillars. Above the roof is an area that probably contains ropes and pulleys for lowering and raising actors and props.

The stage itself has few props and no scenery. There may be a throne for a king, a curtained bed for Juliet, a few stools and tables for interior scenes, and candles or torches to indicate night. Exterior scenes are indicated by the actors' speeches, as in *A Midsummer Night's Dream* when Quince says, "Here's a marvelous place for our rehearsal. This green plot shall be our stage, this hawthorn brake our tiring-house." There are costumes, however, which are the property of the acting company and are not to be worn by the actors when they are not performing.

Such simple equipment enables the acting companies to pack up and tour the countryside when, on occasion, the London theatres are closed because of an outbreak of the plague.

For the moment, however, the day is warm and sunny, and the Globe is filled with an enthusiastic and noisy crowd. Your fellow "groundlings," you notice, reek somewhat of garlic, may not have had a bath recently, and tend to jostle you as they try to find a good viewing spot. But the noise lessens and you forget your surroundings as the first actor steps onto the stage.

CHARACTERS

CHORUS

ESCALUS, *Prince of Verona*

PARIS, *a young count, kinsman to the Prince*

MERCUTIO, *kinsman to the Prince and Romeo's friend*

MONTAGUE

MONTAGUE'S WIFE

ROMEO, *son of the Montagues*

BENVOLIO, *Montague's nephew and Romeo's friend*

CAPULET

CAPULET'S WIFE

JULIET, *daughter of the Capulets*

NURSE

TYBALT, *nephew of Capulet's wife*

PETRUCHIO, *Capulet's kinsman*

SECOND CAPULET, *an old man, Capulet's kinsman*

FRIAR LAURENCE, FRIAR JOHN } *Franciscan friars*

PAGE *to Paris*

ABRAHAM, *servant of the Montagues*

BALTHASAR, *Romeo's servant*

PETER, *servant to the Nurse*

SAMPSON, GREGORY, ANTONY, POTPAN, CLOWN or SERVANT, *Other* SERVANTS } *servants of the Capulets*

APOTHECARY

Three MUSICIANS

Three WATCHMEN

CITIZENS, MASKERS, TORCHBEARERS, GUARDS, *and* ATTENDANTS

SCENE: *Verona; Mantua.*

s.d.* **Chorus** The Chorus, in the form of a sonnet, is spoken by one actor.

3 **mutiny** violence.

6 **star-crossed** ill-fated.

14 **our toil** the actor's efforts.

*stage directions

THE PROLOGUE

Enter CHORUS. n

CHORUS. Two households, both alike in dignity,
In fair Verona, where we lay our scene,
From ancient grudge break to new mutiny,
Where civil blood makes civil hands unclean.
From forth the fatal loins of these two foes
A pair of star-crossed lovers take their life;
Whose misadventured piteous overthrows
Doth with their death bury their parents' strife.
The fearful passage of their death-marked love,
And the continuance of their parents' rage,
Which, but their children's end, naught could remove,
Is now the two hours' traffic of our stage;
The which if you with patient ears attend,
What here shall miss, our toil shall strive to mend.
Exit.

ROMEO & JULIET

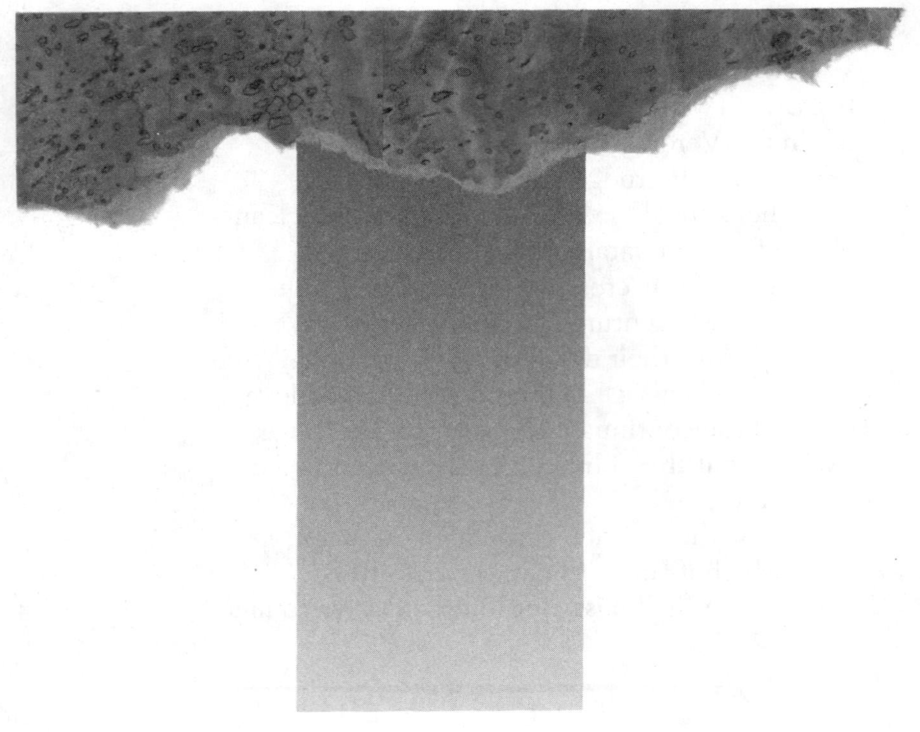

ACT I

"O, she doth teach the torches to burn bright!"

1 **carry coals** be treated as one who does degrading tasks, be insulted.

2 **colliers** those who sell or carry coal. (*Choler* and *collar* in lines 3 and 5 are puns on *collier*.)

3 **an** if; **choler** (kol'ər) anger; **draw** draw swords.

5 **collar** hangman's noose.

13 **take the wall** walk on the side nearest the wall, which is cleaner than the gutter side.

16 **weakest . . . wall** The weakest one is forced to give way.

SCENE 1

Sampson and Gregory, servants of Capulet, meet Abraham and Balthasar, servants to Montague, and they fight. Benvolio tries to stop the fight but is forced to defend himself against Tybalt, who enters with a drawn sword. The quarrel is enlarged by various citizens, and Capulet and Montague, heads of the warring households, threaten to continue the fray. An angry Prince Escalus warns them to end this ancient quarrel on pain of death. When Romeo enters, he talks of his unrequited love for Rosaline.

Verona. A public place.

Enter SAMPSON and GREGORY, *of the house of* CAPULET, *with swords and bucklers.*

SAMPSON. Gregory, on my word, we'll not carry coals. 1

GREGORY. No, for then we should be colliers. 2

SAMPSON. I mean, an we be in choler, we'll draw. 3

GREGORY. Ay, while you live, draw your neck out of
collar. 5

SAMPSON. I strike quickly, being moved.

GREGORY. But thou art not quickly moved to strike.

SAMPSON. A dog of the house of Montague moves me.

GREGORY. To move is to stir, and to be valiant is to stand. Therefore, if thou art moved, thou runn'st away.

SAMPSON. A dog of that house shall move me to stand.
I will take the wall of any man or maid of 13
Montague's.

GREGORY. That shows thee a weak slave, for the
weakest goes to the wall. 16

SAMPSON. 'Tis true, and therefore women, being the weaker vessels, are ever thrust to the wall. Therefore I will push Montague's men from the wall and thrust his maids to the wall.

GREGORY. The quarrel is between our masters and us their men.

33 **Poor John** dried, salted hake, a kind of fish considered a poor kind of food.

38 **Fear** mistrust.

39 **marry** by the Virgin Mary, a mild oath.

44 **bite my thumb** This gesture was considered an insult.

SAMPSON. 'Tis all one. I will show myself a tyrant.
When I have fought with the men, I will be civil
with the maids—I will cut off their heads.

GREGORY. The heads of the maids?

SAMPSON. Ay, the heads of the maids, or their
maidenheads. Take it in what sense thou wilt.

GREGORY. They must take it in sense that feel it.

SAMPSON. Me they shall feel while I am able to stand,
and 'tis known I am a pretty piece of flesh.

GREGORY. 'Tis well thou art not fish; if thou hadst,
thou hadst been Poor John. Draw thy tool. Here 33
comes two of the house of Montagues.

Enter ABRAHAM *and* BALTHASAR.

SAMPSON. My naked weapon is out. Quarrel, I will
back thee.

GREGORY. How? Turn thy back and run?

SAMPSON. Fear me not. 38

GREGORY. No, marry. I fear thee! 39

SAMPSON. Let us take the law of our sides. Let them
begin.

GREGORY. I will frown as I pass by, and let them take it
as they list.

SAMPSON. Nay, as they dare. I will bite my thumb at 44
them, which is a disgrace to them, if they bear it.

ABRAHAM. Do you bite your thumb at us, sir?

SAMPSON. I do bite my thumb, sir.

ABRAHAM. Do you bite your thumb at us, sir?

SAMPSON. (*aside to* GREGORY.) Is the law of our side, if I
say ay?

GREGORY. (*aside to* SAMPSON.) No.

SAMPSON. (*to* ABRAHAM.) No, sir, I do not bite my
thumb at you, sir, but I bite my thumb, sir.

65 **washing** swashing, slashing.

68 **heartless hinds** cowardly rustics or peasants.

s.d. **partisans** long-handled spears.

75 **bills** weapons with hooked blades.

s.d. **gown** dressing gown.

GREGORY. Do you quarrel, sir?

ABRAHAM. Quarrel, sir? No, sir.

SAMPSON. But if you do, sir, I am for you. I serve as good a man as you.

ABRAHAM. No better.

SAMPSON. Well, sir.

Enter BENVOLIO.

GREGORY. (*aside to* SAMPSON.) Say "better." Here comes one of my master's kinsmen.

SAMPSON. (*to* ABRAHAM.) Yes, better, sir.

ABRAHAM. You lie.

SAMPSON. Draw, if you be men. Gregory, remember thy washing blow. (*They fight.*)

BENVOLIO. Part, fools!
Put up your swords. You know not what you do.

Enter TYBALT.

TYBALT. What, art thou drawn among these heartless hinds?
Turn thee, Benvolio, look upon thy death.

BENVOLIO. I do but keep the peace. Put up thy sword,
Or manage it to part these men with me.

TYBALT. What drawn, and talk of peace? I hate the word,
As I hate hell, all Montagues, and thee.
Have at thee, coward! (*They fight.*)

Enter three or four CITIZENS *with clubs or partisans.*

CITIZENS. Clubs, bills, and partisans! Strike! Beat them down!
Down with the Capulets! Down with the Montagues!

Enter old CAPULET *in his gown, and his* WIFE.

CAPULET. What noise is this? Give me my long sword, ho!

s.d. **train** attendants.

84 **Profaners . . . steel** those who defile your weapons with the blood of your neighbors.

95 **Cast . . . ornaments** put aside the staffs appropriate to wise old age.

97 **Cankered . . . cankered** corroded . . . malignant.

s.d. **Exeunt** (ek'sē ənt) They leave.

CAPULET'S WIFE. A crutch, a crutch! Why call you for a sword?

CAPULET. My sword, I say! Old Montague is come
And flourishes his blade in spite of me.

Enter old MONTAGUE *and his* WIFE.

MONTAGUE. Thou villain Capulet!—Hold me not, let me go.

MONTAGUE'S WIFE. Thou shalt not stir one foot to seek a foe.

Enter PRINCE ESCALUS, *with his train.* n

PRINCE ESCALUS. Rebellious subjects, enemies to peace,
Profaners of this neighbor-stainèd steel— 84
Will they not hear? What, ho! You men, you beasts,
That quench the fire of your pernicious rage
With purple fountains issuing from your veins,
On pain of torture, from those bloody hands
Throw your mistempered weapons to the ground,
And hear the sentence of your movèd prince.
Three civil brawls, bred of an airy word,
By thee, old Capulet, and Montague,
Have thrice disturbed the quiet of our streets,
And made Verona's ancient citizens
Cast by their grave-beseeming ornaments, 95
To wield old partisans, in hands as old,
Cankered with peace, to part your cankered hate. 97
If ever you disturb our streets again,
Your lives shall pay the forfeit of the peace.
For this time all the rest depart away.
You, Capulet, shall go along with me;
And Montague, come you this afternoon,
To know our farther pleasure in this case,
To old Freetown, our common judgment-place.
Once more, on pain of death, all men depart.

Exeunt all but MONTAGUE, n
MONTAGUE'S WIFE, *and* BENVOLIO.

106 **new abroach** newly stirred up.

109 **ere** before.

124 **That . . . side** that grows on the west side of the city.

126 **ware** wary.

131 **humor** mood.

138 **Aurora** Roman goddess of dawn.

139 **heavy** sad.

MONTAGUE. Who set this ancient quarrel new abroach? 106
Speak, nephew, were you by when it began?

BENVOLIO. Here were the servants of your adversary,
And yours, close fighting ere I did approach. 109
I drew to part them. In the instant came
The fiery Tybalt, with his sword prepared,
Which, as he breathed defiance to my ears,
He swung about his head and cut the winds,
Who, nothing hurt withal, hissed him in scorn.
While we were interchanging thrusts and blows,
Came more and more, and fought on part and part
Till the prince came, who parted either part.

MONTAGUE'S WIFE. O, where is Romeo? Saw you him today?
Right glad I am he was not at this fray.

BENVOLIO. Madam, an hour before the worshiped sun
Peered forth the golden window of the east,
A troubled mind drave me to walk abroad,
Where, underneath the grove of sycamore
That westward rooteth from the city's side, 124
So early walking did I see your son.
Towards him I made, but he was ware of me 126
And stole into the covert of the wood.
I, measuring his affections by my own,
Which then most sought where most might not be found,
Being one too many by my weary self,
Pursued my humor, not pursuing his, 131
And gladly shunned who gladly fled from me.

MONTAGUE. Many a morning hath he there been seen,
With tears augmenting the fresh morning's dew,
Adding to clouds more clouds with his deep sighs;
But all so soon as the all-cheering sun
Should in the farthest east begin to draw
The shady curtains from Aurora's bed, 138
Away from light steals home my heavy son, 139
And private in his chamber pens himself,

147 **importuned him by any means** pressed him [to tell you] by every possible means.

153 **envious** malicious.

160 **wert . . . stay** were so successful in your waiting.

161 **shrift** confession.

162 **cousin** kinsman.

Shuts up his windows, locks fair daylight out,
And makes himself an artificial night.
Black and portentous must this humor prove,
Unless good counsel may the cause remove.

BENVOLIO. My noble uncle, do you know the cause?

MONTAGUE. I neither know it nor can learn of him.

BENVOLIO. Have you importuned him by any means? 147

MONTAGUE. Both by myself and many other friends.
But he, his own affections' counselor,
Is to himself—I will not say how true—
But to himself so secret and so close,
So far from sounding and discovery,
As is the bud bit with an envious worm 153
Ere he can spread his sweet leaves to the air
Or dedicate his beauty to the sun.
Could we but learn from whence his sorrows grow,
We would as willingly give cure as know.

Enter ROMEO.

BENVOLIO. See where he comes. So please you step aside.
I'll know his grievance, or be much denied.

MONTAGUE. I would thou wert so happy by thy stay 160
To hear true shrift. Come, madam, let's away. 161
Exeunt MONTAGUE *and his* WIFE.

BENVOLIO. Good morrow, cousin.

ROMEO. Is the day so young? 162

BENVOLIO. But new struck nine.

ROMEO. Ay me! Sad hours seem long.
Was that my father that went hence so fast?

BENVOLIO. It was. What sadness lengthens Romeo's hours?

ROMEO. Not having that which, having, makes them short.

171 **Love** Cupid, the Roman god of love; **view** appearance.

173 **muffled** blindfolded (the way Cupid is usually pictured).

174 **will** desire.

185 **coz** cousin, kinsman.

197 **Soft** stop, wait a moment.

BENVOLIO. In love?

ROMEO. Out—

BENVOLIO. Of love?

ROMEO. Out of her favor where I am in love.

BENVOLIO. Alas, that Love, so gentle in his view, 171
Should be so tyrannous and rough in proof!

ROMEO. Alas, that Love, whose view is muffled still, 173
Should without eyes see pathways to his will! 174
Where shall we dine? Oh me! What fray was here?
Yet tell me not, for I have heard it all.
Here's much to do with hate, but more with love.
Why, then, O brawling love, O loving hate!
O any thing of nothing first create!
O heavy lightness, serious vanity,
Misshapen chaos of well-seeming forms,
Feather of lead, bright smoke, cold fire, sick health!
Still-waking sleep, that is not what it is!
This love feel I, that feel no love in this.
Dost thou not laugh?

BENVOLIO. No, coz, I rather weep. 185

ROMEO. Good heart, at what?

BENVOLIO. At thy good heart's oppression.

ROMEO. Why, such is love's transgression.
Griefs of mine own lie heavy in my breast,
Which thou wilt propagate, to have it pressed
With more of thine. This love that thou hast shown
Doth add more grief to too much of mine own.
Love is a smoke raised with the fume of sighs;
Being purged, a fire sparkling in lovers' eyes;
Being vexed, a sea nourished with lovers' tears.
What is it else? A madness most discreet,
A choking gall, and a preserving sweet.
Farewell, my coz.

BENVOLIO. Soft! I will go along. 197
An if you leave me so, you do me wrong.

211 **Dian's** Diana, Roman goddess of chastity.

212 **proof** armor.

214 **stay** submit to.

218 **store** that is, she will leave no children to inherit her beauty.

ROMEO. Tut, I have lost myself. I am not here.
This is not Romeo; he's some other where.

BENVOLIO. Tell me in sadness, who is that you love?

ROMEO. What, shall I groan and tell thee?

BENVOLIO. Groan? Why, no,
But sadly tell me who.

ROMEO. Bid a sick man in sadness make his will.
Ah, word ill urged to one that is so ill!
In sadness, cousin, I do love a woman.

BENVOLIO. I aimed so near when I supposed you loved.

ROMEO. A right good markman! And she's fair I love.

BENVOLIO. A right fair mark, fair coz, is soonest hit.

ROMEO. Well, in that hit you miss. She'll not be hit
With Cupid's arrow. She hath Dian's wit, 211
And, in strong proof of chastity well armed, 212
From love's weak childish bow she lives unharmed.
She will not stay the siege of loving terms, 214
Nor bide th' encounter of assailing eyes,
Nor ope her lap to saint-seducing gold.
O, she is rich in beauty, only poor
That when she dies, with beauty dies her store. 218

BENVOLIO. Then she hath sworn that she will still live chaste?

ROMEO. She hath, and in that sparing makes huge waste;
For beauty starved with her severity
Cuts beauty off from all posterity.
She is too fair, too wise, wisely too fair,
To merit bliss by making me despair.
She hath forsworn to love, and in that vow
Do I live dead, that live to tell it now.

BENVOLIO. Be ruled by me. Forget to think of her.

ROMEO. O, teach me how I should forget to think!

BENVOLIO. By giving liberty unto thine eyes.
Examine other beauties.

231 **To . . . more** to bring her beauty even more to mind.

240 **I'll . . . doctrine** I'll teach you that lesson.

1 **bound** obliged [to keep peace].

4 **reckoning** esteem.

6 **suit** courting.

ROMEO. 'Tis the way
To call hers, exquisite, in question more.
These happy masks that kiss fair ladies' brows,
Being black, put us in mind they hide the fair.
He that is strucken blind cannot forget
The precious treasure of his eyesight lost.
Show me a mistress that is passing fair:
What doth her beauty serve but as a note
Where I may read who passed that passing fair?
Farewell. Thou canst not teach me to forget.

BENVOLIO. I'll pay that doctrine, or else die in debt.
Exeunt.

SCENE 2

Capulet and the County Paris discuss Paris's wish to marry Capulet's daughter. Capulet thinks Juliet too young to marry but gives Paris permission to woo her. He then invites Paris to a party and sends a servant to invite the other guests. When the illiterate sevant asks Romeo to read the names on the guest list, Romeo and Benvolio learn about the party and that Rosaline has been invited. Romeo and Benvolio, though enemies of the Capulets, decide to attend the party, where Benvolio hopes that Romeo will find another woman as fair as Rosaline.

A street.

Enter CAPULET, PARIS, *and the* CLOWN, *a* SERVANT.

CAPULET. But Montague is bound as well as I,
In penalty alike, and 'tis not hard, I think,
For men so old as we to keep the peace.

PARIS. Of honorable reckoning are you both,
And pity 'tis you lived at odds so long.
But now, my lord, what say you to my suit?

15 **earth** body.

18 **she** if she be.

20 **old** traditional.

29 **fennel** herb whose seeds taste like licorice; it was thought to arouse passion.

30 **Inherit** possess.

34 **sirrah** (sir'ə) form of address to a servant or inferior.

39–42 **It . . . nets** The servant mixes the occupations of shoemaker, tailor, fisher, and painter and the tools of their trade. This emphasizes the foolishness of asking an illiterate servant to read a list of names.

CAPULET. But saying o'er what I have said before:
My child is yet a stranger in the world;
She hath not seen the change of fourteen years.
Let two more summers wither in their pride
Ere we may think her ripe to be a bride.

PARIS. Younger than she are happy mothers made.

CAPULET. And too soon marred are those so early made.
The earth hath swallowed all my hopes but she;
She is the hopeful lady of my earth.
But woo her, gentle Paris, get her heart;
My will to her consent is but a part;
And she agreed, within her scope of choice
Lies my consent and fair-according voice.
This night I hold an old accustomed feast,
Whereto I have invited many a guest
Such as I love; and you among the store,
One more, most welcome, makes my number more.
At my poor house look to behold this night
Earth-treading stars that make dark heaven light.
Such comfort as do lusty young men feel
When well-appareled April on the heel
Of limping winter treads, even such delight
Among fresh fennel buds shall you this night
Inherit at my house. Hear all, all see,
And like her most whose merit most shall be;
Which on more view of many, mine, being one,
May stand in number, though in reckoning none.
Come, go with me. (*to the* SERVANT, *giving him a paper.*)
Go, sirrah, trudge about
Through fair Verona; find those persons out
Whose names are written there, and to them say,
My house and welcome on their pleasure stay.

Exit, with PARIS.

SERVANT. Find them out whose names are written here! It is written that the shoemaker should meddle with his yard and the tailor with his last, the fisher with his pencil, and the painter with his

51 **rank** foul.

52 **plaintain leaf** broad leaf of the plantain plant, useful for healing cuts and stings. Romeo is playing on Benvolio's use of *infection*.

55 **bound** tied up.

60 **without book** by memory.

nets; but I am sent to find those persons whose names are here writ, and can never find what names the writing person hath here writ. I must to the learned.—In good time!

Enter BENVOLIO *and* ROMEO.

BENVOLIO. Tut, man, one fire burns out another's
burning,
One pain is lessened by another's anguish;
Turn giddy, and be holp by backward turning;
One desperate grief cures with another's languish.
Take thou some new infection to thy eye,
And the rank poison of the old will die.

ROMEO. Your plaintain leaf is excellent for that.

BENVOLIO. For what, I pray thee?

ROMEO. For your broken shin.

BENVOLIO. Why, Romeo, art thou mad?

ROMEO. Not mad, but bound more than a madman is;
Shut up in prison, kept without my food,
Whipped and tormented and—Good e'en, good
fellow.

SERVANT. God gi' good e'en. I pray, sir, can you read?

ROMEO. Ay, mine own fortune in my misery.

SERVANT. Perhaps you have learned it without book.
But, I pray, can you read anything you see?

ROMEO. Ay, if I know the letters and the language.

SERVANT. Ye say honestly. Rest you merry!
(*He starts to leave.*)

ROMEO. Stay, fellow; I can read. (*reads.*)
"Signor Martino and his wife and daughters,
County Anselme and his beauteous sisters,
The lady widow of Vitruvio,
Signor Placentio and his lovely nieces,
Mercutio and his brother Valentine,
Mine uncle Capulet, his wife, and daughters,

74 **Whither** where.

83 **crush a cup** have a drink.

88 **unattainted** unbiased.

93 **these** that is, Romeo's eyes.

My fair niece Rosaline and Livia,
Signor Valentio and his cousin Tybalt,
Lucio and the lively Helena."
A fair assembly. Whither should they come? 74

SERVANT. Up.

ROMEO. Whither? To supper?

SERVANT. To our house.

ROMEO. Whose house?

SERVANT. My master's.

ROMEO. Indeed, I should have asked thee that before.

SERVANT. Now I'll tell you without asking. My master
is the great rich Capulet; and if you be not of the
house of Montagues, I pray, come and crush a cup 83
of wine. Rest you merry!

Exit.

BENVOLIO. At this same ancient feast of Capulet's
Sups the fair Rosaline whom thou so loves,
With all the admirèd beauties of Verona.
Go thither, and with unattainted eye 88
Compare her face with some that I shall show,
And I will make thee think thy swan a crow.

ROMEO. When the devout religion of mine eye
Maintains such falsehood, then turn tears to fires;
And these who, often drowned, could never die, 93
Transparent heretics, be burnt for liars!
One fairer than my love! The all-seeing sun
Ne'er saw her match since first the world begun.

BENVOLIO. Tut, you saw her fair, none else being by,
Herself poised with herself in either eye;
But in that crystal scales let there be weighed
Your lady's love against some other maid
That I will show you shining at this feast,
And she shall scant show well that now seems best.

ROMEO. I'll go along, no such sight to be shown,
But to rejoice in splendor of mine own.

Exeunt.

8 **give leave** leave us.

14 **teen** sorrow.

16 **Lammastide** the time of Lammas, a harvest festival once held on August 1 in England; **fortnight** two weeks.

18 **Lammas Eve** Juliet's birthday is on July 31.

19 **Susan** apparently the Nurse's deceased child.

SCENE 3

The Nurse, in the presence of Juliet and Capulet's wife, recounts her memories of Juliet's infancy and childhood in repetitious detail. Capulet's wife broaches the subject of Juliet marrying Paris, and Juliet unenthusiastically agrees to consider the idea.

A room in CAPULET'S *house.*

Enter CAPULET'S WIFE *and* NURSE.

WIFE. Nurse, where's my daughter? Call her forth to
me.

NURSE. Now, by my maidenhead at twelve year old,
I bade her come. What, lamb! What, lady-bird!
God forbid! Where's this girl? What, Juliet!

Enter JULIET.

JULIET. How now! Who calls?

NURSE. Your mother.

JULIET. Madam, I am here. What is your will?

WIFE. This is the matter.—Nurse, give leave awhile, 8
We must talk in secret.—Nurse, come back again;
I have remembered me, thou's hear our counsel.
Thou knowest my daughter's of a pretty age.

NURSE. Faith, I can tell her age unto an hour.

WIFE. She's not fourteen.

NURSE. I'll lay fourteen of my teeth,—
And yet, to my teen be it spoken, I have but four,— 14
She's not fourteen. How long is it now
To Lammastide?

WIFE. A fortnight and odd days. 16

NURSE. Even or odd, of all days in the year,
Come Lammas Eve at night shall she be fourteen. 18
Susan and she—God rest all Christian souls!— 19
Were of an age. Well, Susan is with God;

27 **wormwood** bitter herb.

30 **bear a brain** have a good memory.

33 **tetchy** fretful.

34 **"Shake," . . . dovehouse** that is, the dovehouse shook in the earthquake; **trow** (trō) assure you.

35 **trudge** depart.

37 **rood** cross.

39 **broke her brow** cut her forehead.

41 **'A** he.

44 **halidom** holy relic.

49 **stinted** stopped.

54 **cockerel's stone** rooster's testicle.

She was too good for me. But, as I said,
On Lammas Eve at night shall she be fourteen,
That shall she, marry, I remember it well.
'Tis since the earthquake now eleven years;
And she was weaned—I never shall forget it—
Of all the days of the year, upon that day;
For I had then laid wormwood to my dug, 27
Sitting in the sun under the dovehouse wall.
My lord and you were then at Mantua—
Nay, I do bear a brain! But, as I said, 30
When it did taste the wormwood on the nipple
Of my dug and felt it bitter, pretty fool,
To see it tetchy and fall out wi' the dug! 33
"Shake," quoth the dovehouse. 'Twas no need, I trow, 34
To bid me trudge. 35
And since that time it is eleven years;
For then she could stand high-lone; nay, by the rood, 37
She could have run and waddled all about.
For even the day before, she broke her brow, 39
And then my husband—God be with his soul!
'A was a merry man—took up the child. 41
"Yea," quoth he, "dost thou fall upon thy face?
Thou wilt fall backward when thou hast more wit;
Wilt thou not, Jule?" and, by my halidom, 44
The pretty wretch left crying, and said "Ay."
To see now how a jest shall come about!
I warrant, an I should live a thousand years,
I never should forget it. "Wilt thou not, Jule?" quoth he,
And, pretty fool, it stinted, and said "Ay." 49

WIFE. Enough of this. I pray thee, hold thy peace.

NURSE. Yes, madam. Yet I cannot choose but laugh,
To think it should leave crying and say "Ay."
And yet, I warrant, it had upon its brow
A bump as big as a young cockerel's stone, 54
A perilous knock, and it cried bitterly.
"Yea," quoth my husband, "fall'st upon thy face?

69 **thy teat** the teat that you sucked.

73 **much . . . years** at much the same age.

77 **a man of wax** the kind of man one would model in wax; handsome.

79 **Nay** indeed.

84 **married lineament** harmonious facial feature.

85 **content** satisfaction or the contents of a book. (Lines 86–89 contain an extended metaphor comparing Paris to an unbound book and Juliet to the binding.)

90–91 **The fish . . . hide** That is, just as the fish is in its natural element, the fair Juliet would be a suitable or natural "binding" for Paris.

Thou wilt fall backward when thou comest to age,
Wilt thou not, Jule?" It stinted and said "Ay."

JULIET. And stint thou too, I pray thee, Nurse, say I.

NURSE. Peace, I have done. God mark thee to his grace!
Thou wast the prettiest babe that e'er I nursed.
An I might live to see thee married once,
I have my wish.

WIFE. Marry, that "marry" is the very theme
I came to talk of. Tell me, daughter Juliet,
How stands your disposition to be married?

JULIET. It is an honor that I dream not of.

NURSE. An honor? Were not I thine only nurse,
I would say thou hadst sucked wisdom from thy teat.

WIFE. Well, think of marriage now. Younger than you
Here in Verona, ladies of esteem,
Are made already mothers. By my count,
I was your mother much upon these years
That you are now a maid. Thus then in brief:
The valiant Paris seeks you for his love.

NURSE. A man, young lady! Lady, such a man
As all the world—why, he's a man of wax.

WIFE. Verona's summer hath not such a flower.

NURSE. Nay, he's a flower; in faith, a very flower.

WIFE. What say you? Can you love the gentleman?
This night you shall behold him at our feast.
Read o'er the volume of young Paris' face,
And find delight writ there with beauty's pen;
Examine every married lineament,
And see how one another lends content;
And what obscured in this fair volume lies
Find written in the margent of his eyes.
This precious book of love, this unbound lover,
To beautify him, only lacks a cover.
The fish lives in the sea; and 'tis much pride
For fair without the fair within to hide.

98 **if looking liking move** if looking will cause affection.

105 **the County stays** the Count [Paris] waits.

That book in many's eyes doth share the glory,
That in gold clasps locks in the golden story:
So shall you share all that he doth possess,
By having him making yourself no less.

NURSE. No less! Nay, bigger. Women grow by men.

WIFE. Speak briefly, can you like of Paris' love?

JULIET. I'll look to like, if looking liking move; 98
But no more deep will I endart mine eye
Than your consent gives strength to make it fly.

Enter a SERVINGMAN.

SERVINGMAN. Madam, the guests are come, supper served up, you called, my young lady asked for, the Nurse cursed in the pantry, and every thing in extremity. I must hence to wait. I beseech you, follow straight.

WIFE. We follow thee. (*Exit* SERVINGMAN.) Juliet, the County stays. 105

NURSE. Go, girl, seek happy nights to happy days.

Exeunt.

SCENE 4

Romeo, Mercutio, and Benvolio are on their way to Capulet's feast. Romeo protests that he will not take part in the dancing because he is too sad. He then says that he dreamed last night and, in an extended speech, Mercutio says that it is Queen Mab who causes dreams and who makes lovers dream of love. Romeo expresses misgivings about the future.

A street.

Enter ROMEO, MERCUTIO, BENVOLIO, *with five or six other* MASKERS, *and* TORCHBEARERS.

1 **speech** a prepared speech to explain their presence at the party, usually spoken by a messenger.

3 **The date . . . prolixity** Benvolio says that such wordy speeches are out of fashion.

4 **Cupid . . . scarf** Cupid, usually pictured blindfolded (hoodwinked) presented the set speech. (Perhaps a boy was dressed as Cupid.)

5 **Tartar's . . . bow** short, curved bow, like that pictured with Cupid; **lath** thin wood.

6 **crowkeeper** scarecrow.

7 **without-book** memorized.

9 **measure** judge.

10 **measure them a measure** dance a dance with them.

12 **heavy** sad. (*Heavy* is also the opposite of *light* in the same line.)

15 **soles** a pun on *soles* and *soul*.

18 **common bound** ordinary leap, as in a dance, but also referring to "stakes me to the ground" in line 16. See also *bound* in lines 20 and 21.

21 **pitch** height.

23 **And . . . love** If you sink in love, you would be a burden to it.

29 **Give . . . in** Give me a mask (case) to wear.

30 **A visor . . . visor** a mask for an ugly face.

31 **quote** notice.

ROMEO. What, shall this speech be spoke for our excuse? 1
Or shall we on without apology?

BENVOLIO. The date is out of such prolixity: 3
We'll have no Cupid hoodwinked with a scarf, 4
Bearing a Tartar's painted bow of lath, 5
Scaring the ladies like a crowkeeper; 6
Nor no without-book prologue, faintly spoke 7
After the prompter, for our entrance;
But let them measure us by what they will, 9
We'll measure them a measure, and be gone. 10

ROMEO. Give me a torch. I am not for this ambling.
Being but heavy, I will bear the light. 12

MERCUTIO. Nay, gentle Romeo, we must have you dance.

ROMEO. Not I, believe me. You have dancing shoes
With nimble soles; I have a soul of lead 15
So stakes me to the ground I cannot move.

MERCUTIO. You are a lover; borrow Cupid's wings,
And soar with them above a common bound. 18

ROMEO. I am too sore enpiercèd with his shaft
To soar with his light feathers, and so bound
I cannot bound a pitch above dull woe. 21
Under love's heavy burden do I sink.

MERCUTIO. And, to sink in it, should you burden love— 23
Too great oppression for a tender thing.

ROMEO. Is love a tender thing? It is too rough,
Too rude, too boisterous, and it pricks like thorn.

MERCUTIO. If love be rough with you, be rough with love;
Prick love for pricking, and you beat love down.
Give me a case to put my visage in. 29
A visor for a visor! What care I 30
What curious eye doth quote deformities? 31
Here are the beetle brows shall blush for me.

36 **senseless** unfeeling; **rushes** stems of rush plants used for a floor covering.

37 **grandsire phrase** old saying.

38 **candle holder** spectator.

40 **dun's the mouse** that is, keep still, with a pun on *done* in the previous line; **constable's own word** a constable might say "keep still."

41 **If . . . mire** Dun, a grayish brown color, alludes to an old game called "Dun Is in the Mire," in which Dun, a horse, represented by a heavy log, was pulled out of an imaginary mire by the players.

49 **wit** wisdom.

50 **tonight** last night.

57 **atomi** tiny creatures.

BENVOLIO. Come, knock and enter, and no sooner in
But every man betake him to his legs.

ROMEO. A torch for me. Let wantons light of heart
Tickle the senseless rushes with their heels, 36
For I am proverbed with a grandsire phrase: 37
I'll be a candle holder and look on. 38
The game was ne'er so fair, and I am done.

MERCUTIO. Tut, dun's the mouse, the constable's own word. 40
If thou art dun, we'll draw thee from the mire 41
Of—save your reverence—love, wherein thou stickest
Up to the ears. Come, we burn daylight, ho!

ROMEO. Nay, that's not so.

MERCUTIO. I mean, sir, in delay
We waste our lights in vain, like lamps by day.
Take our good meaning, for our judgment sits
Five times in that ere once in our five wits.

ROMEO. And we mean well, in going to this masque
But 'tis no wit to go. 49

MERCUTIO. Why, may one ask?

ROMEO. I dreamt a dream tonight. 50

MERCUTIO. And so did I.

ROMEO. Well, what was yours?

MERCUTIO. That dreamers often lie.

ROMEO. In bed asleep, while they do dream things true.

MERCUTIO. O, then, I see Queen Mab hath been with you.
She is the fairies' midwife, and she comes
In shape no bigger than an agate stone
On the forefinger of an alderman,
Drawn with a team of little atomi 57
Over men's noses as they lie asleep.
Her chariot is an empty hazelnut,

60 **joiner** furniture maker; **grub** insect larva that bores holes in nuts.

62 **spinners'** spiders'.

79 **tithe-pig's** pig given to the parson in place of a tithe or a tenth of one's goods.

81 **benefice** income, living.

84 **breaches** gaps in fortifications; **ambuscadoes** ambushes.

85 **healths** toasts.

90 **elflocks** tangles caused by elves.

Made by the joiner squirrel or old grub, 60
Time out o' mind the fairies' coachmakers.
Her wagon spokes made of long spinners' legs, 62
The cover of the wings of grasshoppers,
Her traces of the smallest spider's web,
Her collars of the moonshine's watery beams,
Her whip of cricket's bone, the lash of film,
Her wagoner a small gray-coated gnat,
Not half so big as a round little worm
Pricked from the lazy finger of a maid.
And in this state she gallops night by night
Through lovers' brains, and then they dream of love;
O'er courtiers' knees, that dream on curtsies straight;
O'er lawyers' fingers who straight dream on fees;
O'er ladies' lips, who straight on kisses dream,
Which oft the angry Mab with blisters plagues
Because their breaths with sweetmeats tainted are.
Sometimes she gallops o'er a courtier's nose.
And then dreams he of smelling out a suit.
And sometime comes she with a tithe-pig's tail 79
Tickling a parson's nose as 'a lies asleep,
Then dreams he of another benefice. 81
Sometime she driveth o'er a soldier's neck,
And then dreams he of cutting foreign throats,
Of breaches, ambuscadoes, Spanish blades, 84
Of healths five fathom deep, and then anon 85
Drums in his ear, at which he starts and wakes,
And being thus frighted swears a prayer or two,
And sleeps again. This is that very Mab
That plats the manes of horses in the night,
And bakes the elflocks in foul sluttish hairs, 90
Which once untangled much misfortune bodes.
This is the hag, when maids lie on their backs,
That presses them and learns them first to bear,
Making them women of good carriage.
This is she—

ROMEO. Peace, peace, Mercutio, peace!
Thou talk'st of nothing.

109 **expire the term** bring to an end.

113 **lusty** lively.

MERCUTIO. True, I talk of dreams;
Which are the children of an idle brain,
Begot of nothing but vain fantasy,
Which is as thin of substance as the air,
And more inconstant than the wind, who woos
Even now the frozen bosom of the north,
And, being angered, puffs away from thence,
Turning his face to the dew-dropping south.

BENVOLIO. This wind you talk of blows us from ourselves.
Supper is done, and we shall come too late.

ROMEO. I fear, too early; for my mind misgives
Some consequence yet hanging in the stars,
Shall bitterly begin his fearful date
With this night's revels, and expire the term
Of a despisèd life closed in my breast,
By some vile forfeit of untimely death.
But He, that hath the steerage of my course,
Direct my sail! On, lusty gentlemen.

BENVOLIO. Strike, drum.
(*They march about the stage and stand to one side.*)

SCENE 5

Capulet warmly welcomes his guests, and Romeo is immediately struck by Juliet's beauty. Tybalt perceives that the masked Romeo is a Montague and wants to kill him. Capulet wants no disturbances and tells Tybalt to be quiet. Juliet responds warmly to Romeo and, when she is called away, Romeo learns from the Nurse that Juliet is a Capulet. Juliet then learns that Romeo is a Montague. Both Romeo and Juliet are dismayed by their discoveries.

A hall in CAPULET'S *house.*

MUSICIANS *waiting. Enter* SERVINGMEN *with napkins.*

2 **trencher** wooden plate.

7 **joint stools** stools made of parts put together by a joiner.

8 **court cupboard** sideboard, place where dishes were kept; **plate** silverware.

9 **marchpane** marzipan, a confection of almonds and sugar.

16–17 **longest liver . . . all** a proverbial expression, "the survivor takes it all."

FIRST SERVINGMAN. Where's Potpan, that he helps not
to take away? He shift a trencher? He scrape a 2
trencher?

SECOND SERVINGMAN. When good manners shall lie all in one or two men's hands, and they unwashed too, 'tis a foul thing.

FIRST SERVINGMAN. Away with the joint stools, remove 7
the court cupboard, look to the plate. Good thou, 8
save me a piece of marchpane; and, as thou lovest 9
me, let the porter let in Susan Grindstone and Nell.
(*Exit* SECOND SERVINGMAN.) Antony, and Potpan!

Enter two more SERVINGMEN.

THIRD SERVINGMAN. Ay, boy, ready.

FIRST SERVINGMAN. You are looked for and called for, asked for and sought for, in the great chamber.

FOURTH SERVINGMAN. We cannot be here and there
too. Cheerly, boys! Be brisk awhile, and the longest 16
liver take all.

Exeunt.

Enter CAPULET, *his* WIFE, JULIET, *and others of his house, meeting the* GUESTS *and* MASKERS.

CAPULET. Welcome, gentlemen! Ladies that have their toes
Unplagued with corns will have a bout with you.
Ah, my mistresses, which of you all
Will now deny to dance? She that makes dainty,
She, I'll swear, hath corns. Am I come near ye now?
Welcome, gentlemen! I have seen the day
That I have worn a visor, and could tell
A whispering tale in a fair lady's ear
Such as would please. 'Tis gone, 'tis gone, 'tis gone.
You are welcome, gentlemen! Come, musicians, play.
(*Music plays, and they dance.*)
A hall, a hall! Give room! And foot it, girls.
(*to* SERVINGMEN.) More light, you knaves; and turn the tables up,

30 **quench the fire** Although the feast takes place in mid-July, a fire may be needed for a cool English summer evening, if not an Italian one.

31 **sirrah** a term usually used for servants; Capulet may be addressing his cousin or, perhaps, himself; **unlooked-for sport** the unexpected arrival of Mercutio and his friends.

38 **Pentecost** seventh Sunday after Easter, but Pentecost does not fall as late as mid-July.

42 **ward** a minor.

49 **dear** precious.

53 **rude** rough.

54 **forswear** renounce any previous oath.

57 **what** how.

58 **antic face** Romeo's grotesque mask.

59 **fleer** jeer; **solemnity** festive time.

And quench the fire; the room is grown too hot. 30
(*to his* COUSIN.) Ah, sirrah, this unlooked-for sport 31
comes well.
Nay, sit, nay, sit, good cousin Capulet,
For you and I are past our dancing days.
How long is't now since last yourself and I
Were in a mask?

SECOND CAPULET. By 'r lady, thirty years.

CAPULET. What, man! 'Tis not so much, 'tis not so
much.
'Tis since the nuptial of Lucentio,
Come Pentecost as quickly as it will, 38
Some five-and-twenty years, and then we masked.

SECOND CAPULET. 'Tis more, 'tis more. His son is elder,
sir;
His son is thirty.

CAPULET. Will you tell me that?
His son was but a ward two years ago. 42

ROMEO. (*to a* SERVINGMAN.) What lady's that, which
doth enrich the hand
Of yonder knight?

SERVINGMAN. I know not, sir.

ROMEO. O, she doth teach the torches to burn bright!
It seems she hangs upon the cheek of night
As a rich jewel in an Ethiop's ear—
Beauty too rich for use, for earth too dear! 49
So shows a snowy dove trooping with crows
As yonder lady o'er her fellows shows.
The measure done, I'll watch her place of stand,
And, touching hers, make blessèd my rude hand. 53
Did my heart love till now? Forswear it, sight! 54
For I ne'er saw true beauty till this night.

TYBALT. This, by his voice, should be a Montague.
Fetch me my rapier, boy. What dares the slave 57
Come hither, covered with an antic face, 58
To fleer and scorn at our solemnity? 59

68 **portly** of good deportment, well-mannered.

76 **semblance** facial expression.

79 **goodman** term referring to someone below the rank of gentleman and thus an insult to Tybalt.

82 **mutiny** disturbance.

83 **set cock-a-hoop** behave recklessly; **be the man** play the big fellow.

86 **scathe** harm; **what** what I am doing.

87 **contrary** oppose.

88 **well said** well done, perhaps said to the dancers; **princox** impertinent boy.

Now, by the stock and honor of my kin,
To strike him dead I hold it not a sin.

CAPULET. Why, how now, kinsman! Wherefore storm
you so?

TYBALT. Uncle, this is a Montague, our foe,
A villain that is hither come in spite
To scorn at our solemnity this night.

CAPULET. Young Romeo is it?

TYBALT. 'Tis he, that villain Romeo.

CAPULET. Content thee, gentle coz, let him alone.
'A bears him like a portly gentleman, 68
And, to say truth, Verona brags of him
To be a virtuous and well-governed youth.
I would not for the wealth of all this town
Here in my house do him disparagement.
Therefore be patient, take no note of him.
It is my will, the which if thou respect,
Show a fair presence and put off these frowns,
An ill-beseeming semblance for a feast. 76

TYBALT. It fits when such a villain is a guest.
I'll not endure him.

CAPULET. He shall be endured.
What, goodman boy? I say, he shall. Go to! 79
Am I the master here, or you? Go to.
You'll not endure him! God shall mend my soul,
You'll make a mutiny among my guests! 82
You will set cock-a-hoop! You'll be the man! 83

TYBALT. Why, uncle, 'tis a shame.

CAPULET. Go to, go to,
You are a saucy boy. Is 't so, indeed?
This trick may chance to scathe you, I know what, 86
You must contrary me! Marry, 'tis time.— 87
Well said, my hearts!—You are a princox, go. 88
Be quiet, or—More light, more light!—For shame!
I'll make you quiet.—What, cheerly, my hearts!

91 **Patience . . . meeting** enforced restraint in the face of anger (choler).

92 **different greeting** opposing mental states (anger and patience).

96 **holy shrine** that is, Juliet's hand.

101 **saints** images of saints.

102 **palmers** pilgrims to the Holy Land who brought back palm branches, a pun on the palm of the hand.

107 **move** take the initiative.

112 **by th' book** by the rule, expertly.

TYBALT. Patience perforce with willful choler meeting 91
Makes my flesh tremble in their different greeting. 92
I will withdraw. But this intrusion shall,
Now seeming sweet, convert to bitterest gall.

Exit.

ROMEO. (*to* JULIET.) If I profane with my unworthiest hand
This holy shrine, the gentle sin is this: 96
My lips, two blushing pilgrims, ready stand
To smooth that rough touch with a tender kiss.

JULIET. Good pilgrim, you do wrong your hand too much,
Which mannerly devotion shows in this;
For saints have hands that pilgrims' hands do touch, 101
And palm to palm is holy palmers' kiss. 102

ROMEO. Have not saints lips, and holy palmers too?

JULIET. Ay, pilgrim, lips that they must use in prayer.

ROMEO. O, then, dear saint, let lips do what hands do.
They pray, grant thou, lest faith turn to despair.

JULIET. Saints do not move, though grant for prayers' sake. 107

ROMEO. Then move not, while my prayer's effect I take.

(*He kisses her.*)

Thus from my lips, by thine, my sin is purged.

JULIET. Then have my lips the sin that they have took.

ROMEO. Sin from my lips? O trespass sweetly urged!

(*He kisses her.*)

Give me my sin again.

JULIET. You kiss by th' book. 112

NURSE. Madam, your mother craves a word with you.

(JULIET *retires.*)

ROMEO. What is her mother?

119 **the chinks** plenty of money.

120 **dear account** expensive reckoning; **My life . . . debt** My life (as Juliet's lover) is owed to my enemy.

121 **The sport . . . best** that is, it is time to leave.

124 **towards** on the way.

126 **honest** honorable.

128 **fay** faith; **waxes** grows.

137 **like** likely.

NURSE. Marry, bachelor,
Her mother is the lady of the house,
And a good lady, and a wise and virtuous.
I nursed her daughter, that you talked withal.
I tell you, he that can lay hold of her
Shall have the chinks.

ROMEO. Is she a Capulet 119
O dear account! My life is my foe's debt. 120

BENVOLIO. Away, be gone! The sport is at the best. 121

ROMEO. Ay, so I fear; the more is my unrest.

CAPULET. Nay, gentlemen, prepare not to be gone.
We have a trifling foolish banquet towards. 124
(A MASKER *whispers in his ear.*)
Is it e'en so? Why, then, I thank you all.
I thank you, honest gentlemen. Good night. 126
More torches here! Come on then, let's to bed.
Ah, sirrah, by my fay, it waxes late. 128
I'll to my rest.
Exeunt all but JULIET *and* NURSE.

JULIET. Come hither, Nurse. What is yond gentleman?

NURSE. The son and heir of old Tiberio.

JULIET. What's he that now is going out of door?

NURSE. Marry, that, I think, be young Petruchio.

JULIET. What's he that follows here, that would not dance?

NURSE. I know not.

JULIET. Go ask his name. (*The* NURSE *leaves.*) If he be married,
My grave is like to be my wedding bed. 137

NURSE. (*returning*) His name is Romeo, and a Montague,
The only son of your great enemy.

JULIET. My only love sprung from my only hate!
Too early seen unknown, and known too late!

142 **Prodigious** ominous.

144 **tis** this.

146 **Anon** that is, we're coming.

Prodigious birth of love it is to me
That I must love a loathèd enemy.

NURSE. What's tis? What's tis?

JULIET. A rhyme I learned even now
Of one I danced withal. (*One calls within* "JULIET.")

NURSE. Anon, anon!
Come let's away. The strangers all are gone.

Exeunt.

ROMEO & JULIET

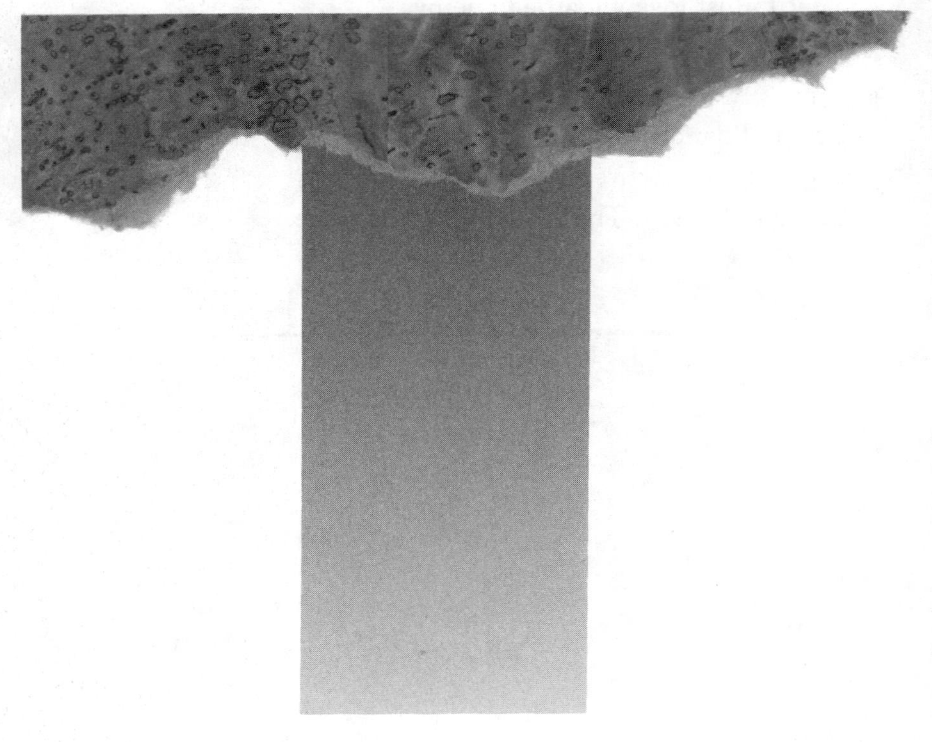

ACT II

"O, that I were a glove upon that hand,
That I might touch that cheek!"

1 **old desire** Romeo's love for Rosaline.

2 **gapes** is eager.

3 **fair** beauty (Rosaline).

10 **use** are accustomed.

14 **Temp'ring extremities . . . sweet** softening their hardship with the pleasure [of their meeting].

2 **dull earth** that is, Romeo's body; **center** that is, Juliet.

PROLOGUE

Enter CHORUS.

CHORUS. Now old desire doth in his deathbed lie,
And young affection gapes to be his heir;
That fair for which love groaned for and would die,
With tender Juliet matched, is now not fair.
Now Romeo is beloved and loves again,
Alike bewitchèd by the charm of looks;
But to his foe supposed he must complain,
And she steal love's sweet bait from fearful hooks,
Being held a foe, he may not have access
To breathe such vows as lovers use to swear;
And she as much in love, her means much less
To meet her now belovèd anywhere,
But passion lends them power, time means, to meet,
Temp'ring extremities with extreme sweet.

Exit.

SCENE 1

Benvolio and Mercutio search for Romeo, who is hidden. Unable to call him forth, the two leave.

Near CAPULET'S *orchard.*

Enter ROMEO, *alone.*

ROMEO. Can I go forward when my heart is here?
Turn back, dull earth, and find thy center out.

Enter BENVOLIO *with* MERCUTIO. ROMEO *retires.*

BENVOLIO. Romeo! My cousin Romeo! Romeo!

MERCUTIO. He is wise,
And, on my life, hath stolen him home to bed.

7 **conjure** summon by magical means.

12 **gossip** friend; **Venus** the goddess of love.

13 **purblind** dim-sighted.

14 **Young Abraham Cupid** perhaps a reference to the biblical Abraham, who lived to be old, and Cupid, depicted as a boy but one of the oldest Roman gods.

15 **When . . . beggar maid.** In an old ballad, the legendary King Cophetua fell in love with and married a beggar maid.

21 **demesnes** regions.

32 **humorous** humid, but also full of moods. (See line 8.)

35 **medlar tree** tree with a small applelike fruit.

40 **truckle bed** bed that can be rolled under another bed.

BENVOLIO. He ran this way, and leapt this orchard wall.
Call, good Mercutio.

MERCUTIO. Nay, I'll conjure too. 7
Romeo! Humors! Madman! Passion! Lover!
Appear thou in the likeness of a sigh.
Speak but one rhyme, and I am satisfied;
Cry but "ay me!" Pronounce but "love" and "dove."
Speak to my gossip Venus one fair word, 12
One nickname for her purblind son and heir, 13
Young Abraham Cupid, he that shot so trim 14
When King Cophetua loved the beggar maid. 15
He heareth not, he stirreth not, he moveth not;
The ape is dead, and I must conjure him.
I conjure thee by Rosaline's bright eyes,
By her high forehead and her scarlet lip,
By her fine foot, straight leg, and quivering thigh,
And the demesnes that there adjacent lie, 21
That in thy likeness thou appear to us!

BENVOLIO. An if he hear thee, thou wilt anger him.

MERCUTIO. This cannot anger him. 'Twould anger him
To raise a spirit in his mistress' circle
Of some strange nature, letting it there stand
Till she had laid it and conjured it down;
That were some spite. My invocation
Is fair and honest; in his mistress' name
I conjure only but to raise up him.

BENVOLIO. Come, he hath hid himself among these trees,
To be consorted with the humorous night. 32
Blind is his love, and best befits the dark.

MERCUTIO. If love be blind, love cannot hit the mark.
Now will he sit under a medlar tree 35
And wish his mistress were that kind of fruit
As maids call medlars when they laugh alone.
O, Romeo, that she were, O, that she were
An open arse and thou a a popering pear!
Romeo, good night. I'll to my truckle bed; 40

6 **thou her maid . . . she** that is, Juliet is fairer than Diana, goddess of the moon.

8 **vestal** virgin.

This field bed is too cold for me to sleep.
Come, shall we go?

BENVOLIO. Go then, for 'tis in vain
To seek him here that means not to be found.
Exeunt BENVOLIO *and* MERCUTIO.

SCENE 2

Romeo comes forward and sees a light at Juliet's window. He overhears her confession of love for him, makes his presence known, and they vow their love for each other. Juliet is called away by the Nurse, but she returns to say that she will send a messenger to him in the morning. Romeo will tell the messenger his arrangements for their marriage. Reluctant to part, they exchange a fond good night.

CAPULET'S *orchard.*

Enter ROMEO.

ROMEO. He jests at scars that never felt a wound.
(JULIET *appears above at a window.*)
But, soft! What light through yonder window breaks?
It is the east, and Juliet is the sun!
Arise, fair sun, and kill the envious moon,
Who is already sick and pale with grief
That thou her maid are far more fair than she, 6
Be not her maid, since she is envious;
Her vestal livery is but sick and green, 8
And none but fools do wear it. Cast it off
It is my lady; O, it is my love!
O, that she knew she were!
She speaks, yet she says nothing. What of that?
Her eye discourses. I will answer it.
I am too bold. 'Tis not to me she speaks.
Two of the fairest stars in all the heaven,

33 **wherefore** why.

39 **though not a Montague** even though you should call yourself something else.

46 **owes** owns.

48 **for** in exchange for.

Having some business, do entreat her eyes
To twinkle in their spheres till they return.
What if her eyes were there, they in her head?
The brightness of her cheek would shame those stars
As daylight doth a lamp; her eyes in heaven
Would through the airy region stream so bright
That birds would sing and think it were not night.
See how she leans her cheek upon her hand!
O, that I were a glove upon that hand,
That I might touch that cheek!

JULIET. Ay me!

ROMEO. She speaks.
O, speak again, bright angel, for thou art
As glorious to this night, being o'er my head,
As is a wingèd messenger of heaven
Unto the white-upturnèd wondering eyes
Of mortals that fall back to gaze on him,
When he bestrides the lazy puffing clouds
And sails upon the bosom of the air.

JULIET. O Romeo, Romeo, wherefore art thou Romeo? 33
Deny thy father and refuse thy name!
Or, if thou wilt not, be but sworn my love,
And I'll no longer be a Capulet.

ROMEO. (*aside*) Shall I hear more, or shall I speak at this?

JULIET. 'Tis but thy name that is my enemy;
Thou art thyself, though not a Montague. 39
What's Montague? It is nor hand, nor foot,
Nor arm, nor face, nor any other part
Belonging to a man. O, be some other name!
What's in a name? That which we call a rose
By any other word would smell as sweet;
So Romeo would, were he not Romeo called,
Retain that dear perfection which he owes 46
Without that title. Romeo, doff thy name,
And for thy name, which is no part of thee, 48
Take all myself.

66 **o'erperch** fly over.

73 **proof** protected.

78 **prorogued** postponed.

ROMEO. I take thee at thy word!
Call me but love, and I'll be new baptized;
Henceforth, I never will be Romeo.

JULIET. What man art thou that, thus bescreened in night
So stumblest on my counsel?

ROMEO. By a name
I know not how to tell thee who I am,
My name, dear saint, is hateful to myself,
Because it is an enemy to thee;
Had I it written, I would tear the word.

JULIET. My ears have yet not drunk a hundred words
Of thy tongue's uttering, yet I know the sound:
Art thou not Romeo and a Montague?

ROMEO. Neither, fair maid, if either thee dislike.

JULIET. How camest thou hither, tell me, and wherefore?
The orchard walls are high and hard to climb,
And the place death, considering who thou art,
If any of my kinsmen find thee here.

ROMEO. With love's light wings did I o'erperch these walls, 66
For stony limits cannot hold love out,
And what love can do, that dares love attempt;
Therefore thy kinsmen are no stop to me.

JULIET. If they do see thee, they will murder thee.

ROMEO. Alack, there lies more peril in thine eye
Than twenty of their swords. Look thou but sweet,
And I am proof against their enmity. 73

JULIET. I would not for the world they saw thee here.

ROMEO. I have night's cloak to hide me from their eyes;
And but thou love me, let them find me here.
My life were better ended by their hate,
Than death proroguèd, wanting of thy love. 78

88 **fain** gladly.

89 **compliment** polite convention.

93 **Jove** chief god of the ancient Romans and god of the heavens; Jupiter.

101 **strange** reserved, distant.

JULIET. By whose direction found'st thou out this
place?

ROMEO. By love, that first did prompt me to inquire.
He lent me counsel, and I lent him eyes.
I am not pilot; yet, wert thou as far
As that vast shore washed with the farthest sea,
I should adventure for such merchandise.

JULIET. Thou know'st the mask of night is on my face,
Else would a maiden blush bepaint my cheek
For that which thou hast heard me speak tonight.
Fain would I dwell on form—fain, fain deny 88
What I have spoke; but farewell compliment! 89
Dost thou love me? I know thou wilt say "Ay,"
And I will take thy word. Yet, if thou swear'st,
Thou mayst prove false. At lovers' perjuries,
They say, Jove laughs. O gentle Romeo, 93
If thou dost love, pronounce it faithfully.
Or if thou thinkest I am too quickly won,
I'll frown and be perverse and say thee nay,
So thou wilt woo, but else not for the world.
In truth, fair Montague, I am too fond,
And therefore thou mayst think my 'havior light.
But trust me, gentleman, I'll prove more true
Than those that have more cunning to be strange. 101
I should have been more strange, I must confess,
But that thou overheard'st, ere I was ware,
My true love passion. Therefore pardon me,
And not impute this yielding to light love,
Which the dark night hath so discoverèd.

ROMEO. Lady, by yonder blessed moon I vow,
That tips with silver all these fruit-tree tops—

JULIET. O, swear not by the moon, th' inconstant
moon,
That monthly changes in her circled orb,
Lest that thy love prove likewise variable.

ROMEO. What shall I swear by?

117 **contract** (kən trakt') exchange of vows.

131 **frank** generous.

JULIET. Do not swear at all,
Or, if thou wilt, swear by the gracious self,
Which is the god of my idolatry,
And I'll believe thee.

ROMEO. If my heart's dear love—

JULIET. Well, do not swear. Although I joy in thee,
I have no joy of this contract tonight. 117
It is too rash, too unadvised, too sudden,
Too like the lightning, which doth cease to be
Ere one can say it lightens. Sweet, good night!
This bud of love, by summer's ripening breath,
May prove a beauteous flower when next we meet.
Good night, good night! As sweet repose and rest
Come to thy heart as that within my breast!

ROMEO. O, wilt thou leave me so unsatisfied?

JULIET. What satisfaction canst thou have tonight?

ROMEO. Th' exchange of thy love's faithful vow for mine.

JULIET. I gave thee mine before thou didst request it:
And yet I would it were to give again.

ROMEO. Wouldst thou withdraw it? For what purpose, love?

JULIET. But to be frank, and give it thee again. 131
And yet I wish but for the thing I have.
My bounty is as boundless as the sea,
My love as deep; the more I give to thee,
The more I have, for both are infinite.
(NURSE *calls within.*)
I hear some noise within. Dear love, adieu!—
Anon, Good nurse!—Sweet Montague, be true.
Stay but a little, I will come again.
Exit.

ROMEO. O blessèd, blessèd night! I am afeared,
Being in night, all this is but a dream,
Too flattering-sweet to be substantial.

143 **bent** inclination.

152 **strife** efforts [to woo me].

160 **tassel-gentle** male falcon.

161 **Bondage . . . aloud** Being in prison requires that one whisper.

162 **tear** (tăr) pierce; **Echo** In mythology, a nymph who pined for Narcissus until only her voice remained.

Enter JULIET, *above*.

JULIET. Three words, dear Romeo, and good night
indeed.
If that thy bent of love be honorable, 143
Thy purpose marriage, send me word tomorrow,
By one that I'll procure to come to thee,
Where and what time thou wilt perform the rite,
And all my fortunes at thy foot I'll lay,
And follow thee my lord throughout the world.

NURSE. (*within*) Madam!

JULIET. I come, anon.—But if thou mean'st not well,
I do beseech thee—

NURSE. (*within*) Madam!

JULIET. By and by, I come—
To cease thy strife, and leave me to my grief. 152
Tomorrow will I send.

ROMEO. So thrive my soul—

JULIET. A thousand times good night!

Exit.

ROMEO. A thousand times the worse, to want thy light.
Love goes toward love as schoolboys from their books,
But love from love, toward school with heavy looks.
(*Retiring slowly*.)

Enter JULIET, *above*.

JULIET. Hist! Romeo, hist! O, for a falconer's voice,
To lure this tassel-gentle back again! 160
Bondage is hoarse, and may not speak aloud, 161
Else would I tear the cave where Echo lies, 162
And make her airy tongue more hoarse than mine
With repetition of "My Romeo!"

ROMEO. It is my soul that calls upon my name.
How silver-sweet sound lovers' tongues by night,
Like softest music to attending ears!

JULIET. Romeo!

168 **nyas** eyas, young falcon, nestling.

178 **wanton** undisciplined child.

180 **gyves** fetters, shackles.

189 **ghostly friar's close cell** spiritual father's narrow room; that is, Friar Laurence's cell in the monastery.

190 **dear hap** good fortune.

ROMEO. My nyas?

JULIET. At what o'clock tomorrow
Shall I send to thee?

ROMEO. By the hour of nine.

JULIET. I will not fail. 'Tis twenty years till then.
I have forgot why I did call thee back.

ROMEO. Let me stand here till thou remember it.

JULIET. I shall forget, to have thee still stand there,
Remembering how I love thy company.

ROMEO. And I'll still stay, to have thee still forget,
Forgetting any other home but this.

JULIET. 'Tis almost morning, I would have thee gone—
And yet no farther than a wanton's bird,
That lets it hop a little from her hand,
Like a poor prisoner in his twisted gyves,
And with a silken thread plucks it back again,
So loving-jealous of his liberty.

ROMEO. I would I were thy bird.

JULIET. Sweet, so would I.
Yet I should kill thee with much cherishing.
Good night, good night! Parting is such sweet sorrow
That I shall say good night till it be morrow.
Exit above.

ROMEO. Sleep dwell upon thine eyes, peace in thy breast!
Would I were sleep and peace, so sweet to rest!
Hence will I to my ghostly friar's close cell,
His help to crave, and my dear hap to tell.
Exit.

4 **from forth** out of the way of; **Titan's fiery wheels** In Greek mythology, the sun god Helios, who begins to drive his chariot across the sky at dawn.

7 **osier cage** willow basket.

8 **baleful** harmful.

11 **children** that is, plants.

14 **None but for some** There are no plants that are not useful for something.

15 **mickle** much.

19 **strained** perverted.

SCENE 3

Friar Laurence, while gathering herbs, muses on the properties, both medicinal and poisonous, of nature's gifts. Romeo enters, tells the surprised Friar of his love for Juliet, and asks the Friar to marry them at once. Thinking that this may end the feud between the warring families, the Friar agrees.

FRIAR LAURENCE'S *cell.*

Enter FRIAR LAURENCE, *with a basket.*

FRIAR LAURENCE. The gray-eyed morn smiles on the frowning night,
Check'ring the eastern clouds with streaks of light,
And fleckled darkness like a drunkard reels
From forth day's path and Titan's fiery wheels. 4
Now, ere the sun advance his burning eye,
The day to cheer and night's dank dew to dry,
I must up-fill this osier cage of ours 7
With baleful weeds and precious-juicèd flowers. 8
The earth that's nature's mother is her tomb;
What is her burying grave, that is her womb;
And from her womb children of divers kind 11
We sucking on her natural bosom find,
Many for many virtues excellent,
None but for some, and yet all different. 14
O, mickle is the powerful grace that lies 15
In plants, herbs, stones, and their true qualities.
For naught so vile that on the earth dove live
But to the earth some special good doth give;
Nor aught so good, but, strained from that fair use, 19
Revolts from true birth, stumbling on abuse.
Virtue itself turns vice, being misapplied,
And vice sometime's by action dignified.

Enter ROMEO.

Within the infant rind of this weak flower
Poison hath residence and medicine power:
For this, being smelt, with that part cheers each part;

26 **stays** stops.

30 **canker** cankerworm.

31 **Benedicite** (ben ə disˈə tā) a blessing on you.

33 **argues** demonstrates; **distempered** disturbed.

45 **ghostly** spiritual.

52 **physic** medicine.

54 **intercession** petition; **steads** helps.

55 **homely** simple.

56 **shrift** absolution, remission of sins granted after confession.

Being tasted, stays all senses with the heart.
Two such opposèd kings encamp them still
In man as well as herbs—grace and rude will;
And where the worser is predominant,
Full soon the canker death eats up that plant.

ROMEO. Good morrow, father.

FRIAR LAURENCE. Benedicite!
What early tongue so sweet saluteth me?
Young son, it argues a distempered head
So soon to bid good morrow to thy bed,
Care keeps his watch in every old man's eye,
And where care lodges, sleep will never lie;
But where unbruisèd youth with unstuffed brain
Doth couch his limbs, there golden sleep doth reign.
Therefore thy earliness doth me assure
Thou art uproused by some distemp'rature;
Or if not so, then here I hit it right,
Our Romeo hath not been in bed tonight.

ROMEO. That last is true; the sweeter rest was mine.

FRIAR LAURENCE. God pardon sin! Wast thou with Rosaline?

ROMEO. With Rosaline, my ghostly father? No.
I have forgot that name and that name's woe.

FRIAR LAURENCE. That's my good son. But where hast thou been, then?

ROMEO. I'll tell thee ere thou ask it me again.
I have been feasting with mine enemy,
Where on a sudden one hath wounded me
That's by me wounded. Both our remedies
Within thy help and holy physic lies.
I bear no hatred, blessèd man, for, lo,
My intercession likewise steads my foe.

FRIAR LAURENCE. Be plain, good son, and homely in thy drift,
Riddling confession finds but riddling shrift.

86 **grace** favor.

88 **did read by rote** repeated trite expressions without understanding them.

ROMEO. Then plainly know my heart's dear love is set
On the fair daughter of rich Capulet.
As mine on hers, so hers is set on mine,
And all combined, save what thou must combine
By holy marriage. When, and where, and how
We met, we wooed and made exchange of vow,
I'll tell thee as we pass; but this I pray,
That thou consent to marry us today.

FRIAR LAURENCE. Holy Saint Francis, what a change is here!
Is Rosaline, that thou didst love so dear,
So soon forsaken? Young men's love then lies.
Not truly in their hearts, but in their eyes.
Jesu Maria, what a deal of brine
Hath washed thy sallow cheeks for Rosaline!
How much salt water thrown away in waste
To season love, that of it doth not taste!
The sun not yet thy sighs from heaven clears,
Thy old groans ring yet in mine ancient ears.
Lo, here upon thy cheek the stain doth sit
Of an old tear that is not washed off yet.
If e'er thou wast thyself and these woes thine,
Thou and these woes were all for Rosaline.
And art thou changed? Pronounce this sentence then:
Women may fall when there's no strength in men.

ROMEO. Thou chid'st me oft for loving Rosaline.

FRIAR LAURENCE. For doting, not for loving, pupil mine.

ROMEO. And bad'st me bury love.

FRIAR LAURENCE. Not in a grave
To lay one in, another out to have.

ROMEO. I pray thee, chide not. She whom I love now
Doth grace for grace and love for love allow. 86
The other did not so.

FRIAR LAURENCE. O, she knew well
Thy love did read by rote, that could not spell. 88

93 **stand** insist.

2 **tonight** last night.

But come, young waverer, come, go with me,
In one respect, I'll thy assistant be;
For this alliance may so happy prove
To turn your households' rancor to pure love.

ROMEO. O, let us hence! I stand on sudden haste. 93

FRIAR LAURENCE. Wisely and slow. They stumble that run fast.

Exeunt.

SCENE 4

Benvolio and Mercutio still search for Romeo. Benvolio reveals that Tybalt has sent a letter to Romeo's father, and Mercutio assumes that it is a challenge to a duel. When Romeo enters, he and Mercutio banter good-naturedly. The Nurse enters with her servant Peter, and Mercutio jests with her as well, which offends her. As Mercutio and Benvolio leave, Romeo asks the Nurse to tell Juliet to meet him at Friar Laurence's cell that afternoon. He further says that his servant will give the Nurse a rope ladder, which she must keep secret.

A street in Verona.

Enter BENVOLIO *and* MERCUTIO.

MERCUTIO. Where the devil should this Romeo be?
Came he not home tonight? 2

BENVOLIO. Not to his father's. I spoke with his man.

MERCUTIO. Why, that same pale hardhearted wench, that Rosaline,
Torments him so that he will sure run mad.

BENVOLIO. Tybalt, the kinsman to old Capulet,
Hath sent a letter to his father's house.

MERCUTIO. A challenge, on my life.

BENVOLIO. Romeo will answer it.

15 **pin** center of a target.

16 **cleft** split; **blind bow-boy's butt shaft** Cupid's blunt arrow.

19 **prince of cats** In the stories of Reynard the Fox, Tybert or Tybalt was the name of the cat.

21 **prick song** music written out or "pricked."

22 **proportion** rhythm.

25 **first house** best school of fencing.

26 ***passado*** forward thrust; ***punto reverso*** backhanded stroke; ***hay*** thrust through.

29 **phantasimes** fops; **new tuners of accents** those who use new foreign words.

33 **flies** parasites.

36 **bones** bodies, with a pun on the French *bon*, "good."

38 **roe** deer, with a pun on the first syllable of Romeo's name. (He is only partly there.)

40 **numbers** verse; **Petrarch . . . Laura** Petrarch, an Italian Renaissance poet, addressed his sonnets to Laura.

42–44 **Dido . . . Thisbe** other famous women in literature. Mercutio is jesting that they were as nothing compared to Rosaline.

MERCUTIO. Any man that can write may answer a letter.

BENVOLIO. Nay, he will answer the letter's master, how he dares, being dared.

MERCUTIO. Alas poor Romeo! He is already dead,
stabbed with a white wench's black eye, run
through the ear with a love song, the very pin of his 15
heart cleft with the blind bow-boy's butt shaft. And 16
is he a man to encounter Tybalt?

BENVOLIO. Why, what is Tybalt?

MERCUTIO. More than prince of cats. O, he's the 19
courageous captain of compliments. He fights as
you sing prick song, keeps time, distance and 21
proportion; he rests his minim rests, one, two, and 22
the third in your bosom. The very butcher of a silk
button, a duellist, a duellist; a gentlemen of the
very first house, of the first and second cause. Ah, 25
the immortal *passado*! The *punto reverso*! The *hay*! 26

BENVOLIO. The what?

MERCUTIO. The pox of such antic, lisping, affecting,
phantasimes, these new tuners of accents! "By Jesu, 29
a very good blade! A very tall man! A very good
whore!" Why, is not this a lamentable thing,
grandsire, that we should be thus afflicted with
these strange flies, these fashionmongers, these 33
pardon-me's, who stand so much on the new form
that they cannot sit at ease on the old bench? O,
their bones, their bones! 36

Enter ROMEO.

BENVOLIO. Here comes Romeo, here comes Romeo.

MERCUTIO. Without his roe, like a dried herring. O 38
flesh, flesh, how art thou fishified! Now is he for
the numbers that Petrarch flowed in. Laura, to his 40
lady, was but a kitchen wench—marry, she had a
better love to berhyme her—Dido a dowdy, 42

43 **hildings** good-for-nothings.

46 **to your French slop** appropriate to your attire, loose French trousers.

47 **counterfeit** slip. Counterfeit coins were called *slips*.

51 **conceive** understand.

56 **bow in the hams** curtsy.

60 **pink** perfection. There follows a series of puns on *pink*, the flower, and *pink*, the perforated ornaments on a shoe (pump), which lead to puns on *sole* (of a shoe) and *solely* (singular).

72 **Switch and spurs** that is, keep up the pace. (A horse would be encouraged by a switch and spurs.)

73 **match** victory.

Cleopatra a gipsy, Helen and Hero, hildings and 43
harlots, Thisbe, a gray eye or so, but not to the
purpose. Signor Romeo, bonjour! There's a French
salutation to your French slop. You gave us the 46
counterfeit fairly last night. 47

ROMEO. Good morrow to you both. What counterfeit did I give you?

MERCUTIO. The slip, sir, the slip. Can you not
conceive? 51

ROMEO. Pardon, good Mercutio, my business was great, and in such a case as mine a man may strain courtesy.

MERCUTIO. That's as much as to say, such a case as
yours constrains a man to bow in the hams. 56

ROMEO. Meaning, to curtsy.

MERCUTIO. Thou hast most kindly hit it.

ROMEO. A most courteous exposition.

MERCUTIO. Nay, I am the very pink of courtesy. 60

ROMEO. Pink for flower.

MERCUTIO. Right.

ROMEO. Why, then is my pump well flowered.

MERCUTIO. Sure wit, follow me this jest now till thou hast worn out thy pump, that when the single sole of it is worn, the jest may remain, after the wearing, solely singular.

ROMEO. O single-soled jest, solely singular for the singleness!

MERCUTIO. Come between us, good Benvolio. My wits faint.

ROMEO. Switch and spurs, switch and spurs! Or I'll cry 72
a match. 73

MERCUTIO. Nay, if our wits run the wild-goose chase, I am done, for thou hast more of the wild goose in

82 **sweeting** sweet apple.

86 **cheveril** kid leather.

87 **ell** unit of measurement, forty-five inches.

95 **natural** idiot, fool.

96 **bauble** a carved stick once carried by a court jester or fool.

105 **goodly gear** matter for mockery.

one of thy wits than, I am sure, I have in my whole five. Was I with you there for the goose?

ROMEO. Thou wast never with me for anything when thou wast not there for the goose.

MERCUTIO. I will bite thee by the ear for that jest.

ROMEO. Nay, good goose, bite not.

MERCUTIO. Thy wit is a very bitter sweeting; it is a 82
most sharp sauce.

ROMEO. And is it not, then, well served in to a sweet goose?

MERCUTIO. O, here's a wit of cheveril, that stretches 86
from an inch narrow to an ell broad! 87

ROMEO. I stretch it out for that word "broad," which added to the goose, proves thee far and wide a broad goose.

MERCUTIO. Why, is not this better now than groaning
for love? Now art thou sociable, now art thou
Romeo; now art thou what thou art, by art as well
as by nature. For this driveling love is like a great
natural that runs lolling up and down to hide his 95
bauble in a hole. 96

BENVOLIO. Stop there, stop there.

MERCUTIO. Thou desirest me to stop in my tale against the hair.

BENVOLIO. Thou wouldst else have made thy tale large.

MERCUTIO. O, thou art deceived; I would have made it short, for I was come to the whole depth of my tale and meant indeed to occupy the argument no longer.

ROMEO. Here's goodly gear! 105

Enter NURSE *and* PETER.

A sail, a sail!

BENVOLIO. Two, two; a shirt and a smock.

119–120 **One . . . mar** a man made in God's image but who mars himself by sinning.

121 **troth** faith.

122 **quoth 'a** said he.

131 **confidence** The Nurse may mean "conference."

136–137 **hare** slang for "prostitute"; **lenten pie** pie without meat in observance of Lent, the season before Easter.

137 **hoar** moldy, with a pun on "whore."

NURSE. Peter!

PETER. Anon!

NURSE. My fan, Peter.

MERCUTIO. Good Peter, to hide her face, for her fan's the fairer of the two.

NURSE. God gi' good morrow, gentlemen.

MERCUTIO. God gi' good e'en, fair gentlewoman.

NURSE. Is it good e'en?

MERCUTIO. 'Tis no less, I tell ye; for the bawdy hand of the dial is now upon the prick of noon.

NURSE. Out upon you! What a man are you?

ROMEO. One, gentlewoman, that God hath made—for 119
himself to mar.

NURSE. By my troth, it is well said, "For himself to 121
mar," quoth 'a? Gentlemen, can any of you tell me 122
where I may find the young Romeo?

ROMEO. I can tell you; but young Romeo will be older when you have found him than he was when you sought him. I am the youngest of that name, for fault of a worse.

NURSE. You say well.

MERCUTIO. Yea, is the worst well? Very well took, i' faith, wisely, wisely.

NURSE. If you be he, sir, I desire some confidence with 131
you.

BENVOLIO. She will indite him to some supper.

MERCUTIO. A bawd, a bawd, a bawd! So ho!

ROMEO. What hast thou found?

MERCUTIO. No hare, sir, unless a hare, sir, in a lenten 136
pie, that is something stale and hoar ere it be spent. 137
(*He sings.*)

150 **ropery** roguery, rascality.

153 **stand to** abide by.

157 **flirt-gills** loose women.

158 **skains-mates** perhaps, outlaws' mates.

An old hare hoar,
And an old hare hoar,
Is very good meat in Lent,
But a hare that is hoar,
Is too much for a score,
When it hoars ere it be spent.

Romeo, will you come to your father's? We'll to dinner thither.

ROMEO. I will follow you.

MERCUTIO. Farewell, ancient lady. Farewell, (*singing*) "lady, lady, lady."

Exeunt MERCUTIO *and* BENVOLIO.

NURSE. I pray you, sir, what saucy merchant was this,
that was so full of his ropery? 150

ROMEO. A gentleman, Nurse, that loves to hear himself
talk, and will speak more in a minute than he will
stand to in a month. 153

NURSE. An 'a speak anything against me, I'll take him
down, an 'a were lustier than he is, and twenty such
Jacks; and if I cannot, I'll find those that shall.
Scurvy knave! I am none of his flirt-gills; I am none 157
of his skains-mates. (*to* PETER.) And thou must 158
stand by too, and suffer every knave to use me at
his pleasure!

PETER. I saw no man use you at his pleasure. If I had, my weapon should quickly have been out; I warrant you, I dare draw as soon as another man, if I see occasion in a good quarrel and the law on my side.

NURSE. Now, afore God, I am so vexed that every part about me quivers. Scurvy knave! Pray you, sir, a word; and as I told you, my young lady bade me inquire you out. What she bid me say, I will keep to myself. But first let me tell ye, if ye should lead her in a fool's paradise, as they say, it were a very gross kind of behavior, as they say. For the gentlewoman

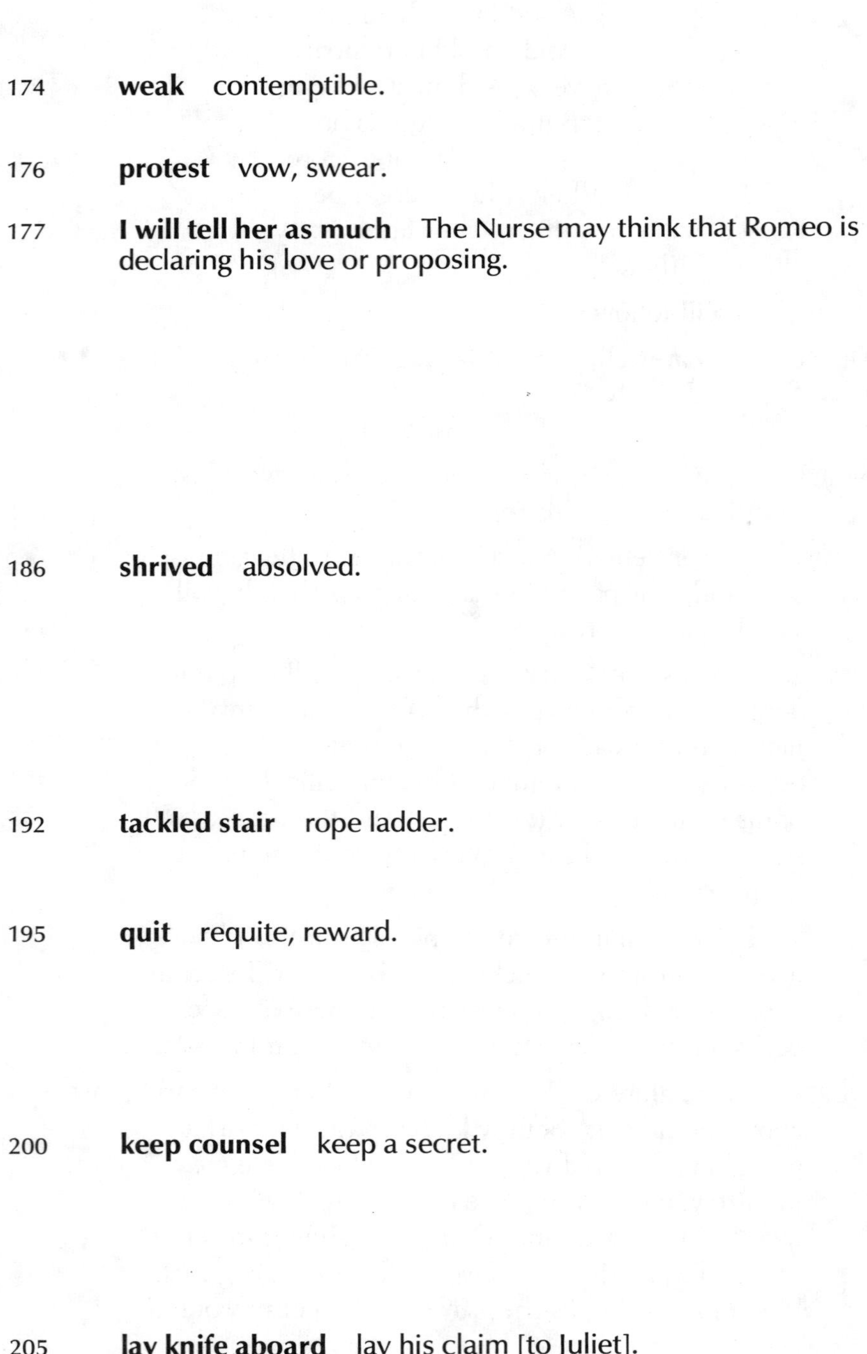

174 **weak** contemptible.

176 **protest** vow, swear.

177 **I will tell her as much** The Nurse may think that Romeo is declaring his love or proposing.

186 **shrived** absolved.

192 **tackled stair** rope ladder.

195 **quit** requite, reward.

200 **keep counsel** keep a secret.

205 **lay knife aboard** lay his claim [to Juliet].

is young, and therefore, if you should deal double with her, truly it were an ill thing to be offered to any gentlewoman, and very weak dealing.

ROMEO. Nurse, commend me to thy lady and mistress. I protest unto thee—

NURSE. Good heart, and i' faith, I will tell her as much. Lord, Lord, she will be a joyful woman.

ROMEO. What wilt thou tell her, Nurse? Thou dost not mark me.

NURSE. I will tell her, sir, that you do protest, which, as I take it, is a gentlemanlike offer.

ROMEO. Bid her devise
Some means to come to shrift this afternoon,
And there she shall at Friar Laurence' cell
Be shrived and married. Here is for thy pains.

NURSE. No, truly, sir; not a penny.

ROMEO. Go to, I say you shall.

NURSE. This afternoon, sir? Well, she shall be there.

ROMEO. And stay, good Nurse, behind the abbey wall.
Within this hour my man shall be with thee,
And bring thee cords made like a tackled stair,
Which to the high topgallant of my joy
Must be my convoy in the secret night.
Farewell. Be trusty, and I'll quit thy pains.
Farewell. Commend me to thy mistress.

NURSE. Now God in heaven bless thee! Hark you, sir.

ROMEO. What say'st thou, my dear Nurse?

NURSE. Is your man secret? Did you ne'er hear say,
"Two may keep counsel, putting one away"?

ROMEO. Warrant thee, my man's as true as steel.

NURSE. Well, sir, my mistress is the sweetest lady—Lord, Lord! When 'twas a little prating thing—O, there is a nobleman in town, one Paris, that would fain lay knife aboard; but she, good soul, had as lief

209 **clout in the versal** cloth in the universal.

212 **dog's name** The sound of the letter *R* was thought to suggest a dog's growl.

214 **sentential** the Nurse may mean "sentences."

219 **Before, and apace** go before me quickly.

see a toad, a very toad, as see him. I anger her
sometimes, and tell her that Paris is the properer
man, but I'll warrant you, when I say so, she looks
as pale as any clout in the versal world. Doth not 209
rosemary and Romeo begin both with a letter?

ROMEO. Ay, Nurse, what of that? Both with an R.

NURSE. Ah, mocker! That's the dog's name; R is for the 212
—No; I know it begins with some other letter—
and she hath the prettiest sententious of it, of you 214
and rosemary, that is would do you good to hear it.

ROMEO. Commend me to thy lady.

NURSE. Ay, a thousand times. (*Exit* ROMEO.) Peter!

PETER. Anon!

NURSE. Before, and apace. 219

Exeunt.

SCENE 5

Juliet impatiently awaits the Nurse's return. When the Nurse arrives she complains of her aches before conveying Romeo's message, much to Juliet's frustration. When she finally reveals that Juliet is to meet Romeo and that he will then climb to her window after dark, Juliet is ecstatic.

CAPULET'S *orchard.*

Enter JULIET.

JULIET. The clock struck nine when I did send the
Nurse:
In half an hour she promised to return.
Perchance she cannot meet him. That's not so.
O, she is lame! Love's heralds should be thoughts,
Which ten times faster glides than the sun's beams
Driving back shadows over louring hills,

14 **bandy** toss back and forth.

16 **feign as** act as though.

25 **give me leave** let me alone.

36 **stay the circumstance** await the details.

Therefore do nimble-pinioned doves draw Love,
And therefore hath the wind-swift Cupid wings.
Now is the sun upon the highmost hill
Of this day's journey, and from nine till twelve
Is three long hours, yet she is not come.
Had she affections and warm youthful blood,
She would be as swift in motion as a ball;
My words would bandy her to my sweet love,
And his to me.
But old folks, many feign as they were dead—
Unwieldy, slow, heavy, and pale as lead.

Enter NURSE *and* PETER.

O God, she comes! O honey Nurse, what news?
Hast thou met with him? Send thy man away.

NURSE. Peter, stay at the gate.

Exit PETER.

JULIET. Now, good sweet nurse,—O Lord, why lookest thou sad?
Though news be sad, yet tell them merrily;
If good, thou shamest the music of sweet news
By playing it to me with so sour a face.

NURSE. I am aweary; give me leave awhile.
Fie, how my bones ache! What a jaunce have I had!

JULIET. I would thou hadst my bones and I thy news.
Nay, come, pray thee, speak. Good, good Nurse, speak.

NURSE. Jesu, what haste! Can you not stay awhile?
Do you not see that I am out of breath?

JULIET. How art thou out of breath, when thou hast breath
To say to me that thou art out of breath?
The excuse that thou dost make in this delay
Is longer than the tale thou dost excuse.
Is thy news good or bad? Answer to that;
Say either, and I'll stay the circumstance:
Let me be satisfied: is 't good or bad?

52 **Beshrew** curse.

66 **coil** fuss, trouble.

NURSE. Well, you have made a simple choice. You know not how to choose a man. Romeo? No, not he. Though his face be better than any man's, yet his leg excels all men's; and for a hand, and a foot, and a body, though they be not to be talked on, yet they are past compare. He is not the flower of courtesy, but, I'll warrant him, as gentle as a lamb. Go thy ways, wench. Serve God. What, have you dined at home?

JULIET. No, no; but all this did I know before.
What says he of our marriage? What of that?

NURSE. Lord, how my head aches! What a head have I!
It beats as it would fall in twenty pieces.
My back o' t' other side—ah, my back, my back!
Beshrew your heart for sending me about 52
To catch my death with jauncing up and down!

JULIET. I' faith, I am sorry that thou art not well.
Sweet, sweet, sweet Nurse, tell me, what says my love?

NURSE. Your love says, like an honest gentleman, and a courteous, and a kind, and a handsome, and I warrant, a virtuous—Where is your mother?

JULIET. Where is my mother? Why, she is within.
Where should she be? How oddly thou repliest!
"Your love says, like an honest gentleman,
Where is your mother?"

NURSE. O God's Lady dear!
Are you so hot? Marry, come up, I trow.
Is this the poultice for my aching bones?
Henceforward do your messages yourself.

JULIET. Here's such a coil! Come, what says Romeo? 66

NURSE. Have you got leave to go to shrift today?

JULIET. I have.

NURSE. Then hie you hence to Friar Laurence's cell;
There stays a husband to make you a wife,

4 **countervail** outweigh.

6 **close** join.

Now comes the wanton blood up in your cheeks,
They'll be in scarlet straight at any news.
Hie you to church; I must another way,
To fetch a ladder, by the which your love
Must climb a bird's nest soon when it is dark.
I am the drudge, and toil in your delight,
But you shall bear the burden soon at night.
Go. I'll to dinner. Hie you to the cell.

JULIET. Hie to high fortune! Honest Nurse, farewell.

Exeunt.

SCENE 6

Juliet meets Romeo at Friar Laurence's cell and the Friar prepares to marry them.

FRIAR LAURENCE'S *cell.*

Enter FRIAR LAURENCE *and* ROMEO.

FRIAR LAURENCE. So smile the heavens upon this holy act
That after-hours with sorrow chide us not!

ROMEO. Amen, amen! But come what sorrow can,
It cannot countervail the exchange of joy 4
That one short minute gives me in her sight,
Do thou but close our hands with holy words, 6
Then love-devouring death do what he dare;
It is enough I may but call her mine.

FRIAR LAURENCE. These violent delights have violent ends
And in their triumph die, like fire and powder,
Which as they kiss consume. The sweetest honey

12 **his** its.

13 **confounds** destroys.

20 **vanity** empty delight.

25 **that** if.

26 **blazon it** set it forth.

30 **Conceit** true understanding.

31 **Brags of** boasts of.

Is loathsome in his own deliciousness,
And in the taste confounds the appetite.
Therefore, love moderately. Long love doth so;
Too swift arrives as tardy as too slow.

Enter JULIET.

Here comes the lady. O, so light a foot
Will ne'er wear out the everlasting flint.
A lover may bestride the gossamers
That idles in the wanton summer air,
And yet not fall; so light is vanity.

JULIET. Good even to my ghostly confessor.

FRIAR LAURENCE. Romeo shall thank thee, daughter, for us both.

JULIET. As much to him, else is his thanks too much.

ROMEO. Ah, Juliet, if the measure of thy joy
Be heaped like mine, and that thy skill be more
To blazon it, then sweeten with thy breath
This neighbor air, and let rich music's tongue
Unfold the imagined happiness that both
Receive in either by this dear encounter.

JULIET. Conceit, more rich in matter than in words,
Brags of his substance, not of ornament,
They are but beggars that can count their worth,
But my true love is grown to such excess
I cannot sum up sum of half my wealth.

FRIAR LAURENCE. Come, come with me, and we will make short work;
For, by your leaves, you shall not stay alone
Till Holy Church incorporate two in one.

Exeunt.

ROMEO & JULIET

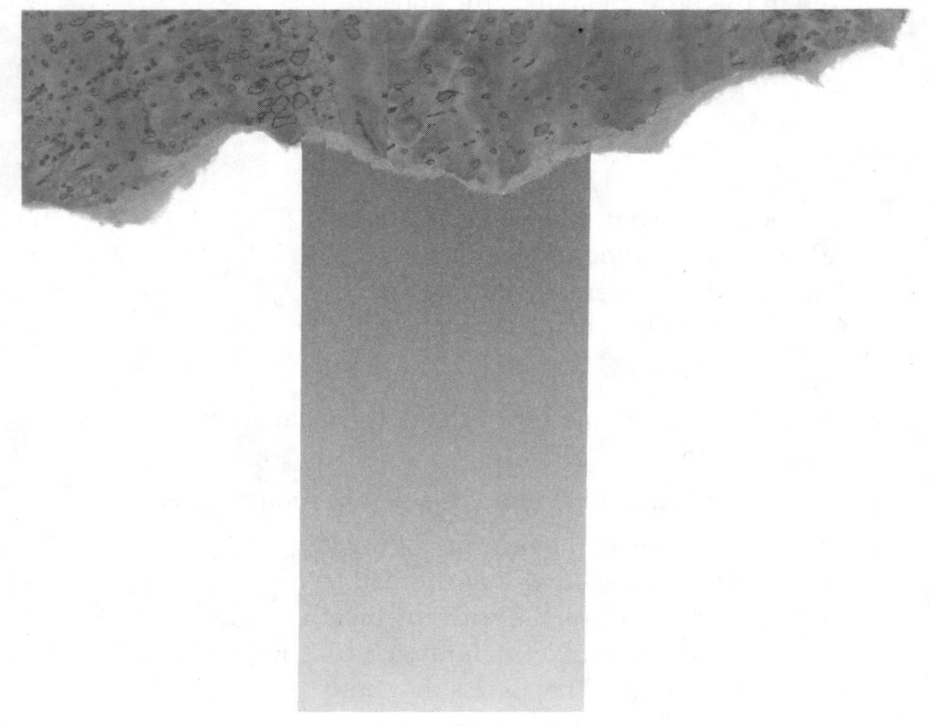

ACT III

". . . A plague o' both your houses!"

2 **Capels** Capulets.

9 **drawer** person who draws drink, tavern keeper.

SCENE 1

Benvolio and Mercutio meet Tybalt, and Mercutio taunts Tybalt. When Romeo enters, Tybalt challenges him to a duel. When Romeo refuses, Mercutio draws his sword. Romeo tries to prevent the fight, but Tybalt stabs Mercutio and runs away. Mercutio is helped off by Benvolio, who returns to say that Mercutio is dead. Tybalt returns and Romeo avenges Mercutio's death by killing Tybalt. Benvolio urges Romeo to flee, and Romeo does so as Escalus enters with Montagues and Capulets and demands to know who started the fight. Benvolio relates what happened, and Escalus banishès the absent Romeo from Verona.

A public place.

Enter MERCUTIO, BENVOLIO, PAGE, *and* SERVANTS.

BENVOLIO. I pray thee, good Mercutio, let's retire.
The day is hot, the Capels abroad, 2
And if we meet we shall not scape a brawl;
For now these hot days is the mad blood stirring.

MERCUTIO. Thou art like one of those fellows that,
when he enters the confines of a tavern, claps me
his sword upon the table and says "God send me no
need of thee!" and by the operation of the second
cup draws it on the drawer, when indeed there is 9
no need.

BENVOLIO. Am I like such a fellow?

MERCUTIO. Come, come, thou art as hot a Jack in thy mood as any in Italy, and as soon moved to be moody, and as soon moody to be moved.

BENVOLIO. And what to?

MERCUTIO. Nay, an there were two such, we should have none shortly, for one would kill the other. Thou! Why, thou wilt quarrel with a man that hath a hair more or a hair less in his beard than thou hast. Thou wilt quarrel with a man for cracking nuts, having no other reason but because thou hast hazel eyes. What eye but such an eye would spy out such a quarrel? Thy head is as full of quarrels as an egg is full of meat, and yet thy head hath been

29 **doublet** jacket.

34 **fee simple** absolute possession.

34–35 **for an hour and a quarter** that is, I would be dead before that time.

36 **simple** stupid.

minstrels Tybalt uses *consortest* to mean "keep company with." Mercutio deliberately takes it to mean "play together" as musicians (minstrels) would.

fiddlestick Mercutio uses the word to refer to his sword.

beaten as addle as an egg for quarreling. Thou hast
quarreled with a man for coughing in the street,
because he hath wakened thy dog that hath lain
asleep in the sun. Didst thou not fall out with a
tailor for wearing his new doublet before Easter? 29
With another, for tying his new shoes with old
ribbon? And yet thou wilt tutor me from
quarreling!

BENVOLIO. An I were so apt to quarrel as thou art, any
man should buy the fee simple of my life for an 34
hour and a quarter.

MERCUTIO. The fee simple! O simple! 36

Enter TYBALT *and others.*

BENVOLIO. By my head, here come the Capulets.

MERCUTIO. By my heel, I care not.

TYBALT. Follow me close, for I will speak to them.
Gentlemen, good e'en. A word with one of you.

MERCUTIO. And but one word with one of us? Couple it
with something: make it a word and a blow.

TYBALT. You shall find me apt enough to that, sir, an
you will give me occasion.

MERCUTIO. Could you not take some occasion without
giving?

TYBALT. Mercutio, thou consortest with Romeo.

MERCUTIO. Consort? What, dost thou make us
minstrels? An thou make minstrels of us, look to 49
hear nothing but discords. Here's my fiddlestick; 50
here's that shall make you dance. 'Zounds, consort!

BENVOLIO. We talk here in the public haunt of men.
Either withdraw into some private place,
Or reason coldly of your grievances,
Or else depart; here all eyes gaze on us.

MERCUTIO. Men's eyes were made to look, and let them
gaze.
I will not budge for no man's pleasure, I.

58–59 **your livery** the uniform of your servants. Mercutio takes "my man" in line 58 to mean "my servant."

60 **field** place for a duel.

61 **your worship** polite title, used here in mockery.

65 **excuse . . . rage** excuse my not showing the anger that would be appropriate.

71 **devise** imagine.

73 **tender** value.

76 ***Alla stoccado*** a fencing term for "at the thrust," here an insulting nickname for Tybalt; **carries it away** wins.

81 **dry-beat** beat roundly but without drawing blood.

82 **pilcher** scabbard, the sheath for a sword.

Enter ROMEO.

TYBALT. Well, peace be with you, sir. Here comes my
man. 58

MERCUTIO. But I'll be hanged, sir, if he wear your
livery.
Marry, go before to field, he'll be your follower; 60
Your worship in that sense may call him man. 61

TYBALT. Romeo, the love I bear thee can afford
No better term than this: thou art a villain.

ROMEO. Tybalt, the reason that I have to love thee
Doth much excuse the appertaining rage 65
To such a greeting. Villain am I none.
Therefore, farewell. I see thou know'st me not.

TYBALT. Boy, this shall not excuse the injuries
That thou hast done me. Therefore turn and draw.

ROMEO. I do protest I never injured thee.
But love thee better than thou canst devise 71
Till thou shalt know the reason of my love.
And so, good Capulet—which name I tender 73
As dearly as mine own—be satisfied.

MERCUTIO. O calm, dishonorable, vile submission!
Alla stoccado carries it away. (*He draws.*) 76
Tybalt, you ratcatcher, will you walk?

TYBALT. What wouldst thou have with me?

MERCUTIO. Good king of cats, nothing but one of your
nine lives, that I mean to make bold withal, and, as
you shall use me hereafter, dry-beat the rest of the 81
eight. Will you pluck your sword out of his pilcher 82
by the ears? Make haste, lest mine be about your
ears ere it be out.

TYBALT. I am for you. (*He draws.*)

ROMEO. Gentle Mercutio, put thy rapier up.

MERCUTIO. Come, sir, your *passado*. (*They fight.*)

ROMEO. Draw, Benvolio; beat down their weapons.
Gentlemen, for shame, forbear this outrage!

105 **by the book of arithmetic** by the numbers, by the rules of fencing.

113 **ally** relative.

119 **temper** state of mind.

Tybalt, Mercutio, the Prince expressly hath
Forbid this bandying in Verona streets.
Hold, Tybalt! Good Mercutio!

(TYBALT *under* ROMEO'S *arm stabs* MERCUTIO *and flies with his followers.*)

MERCUTIO. I am hurt.
A plague o'both your houses! I am sped.
Is he gone, and hath nothing?

BENVOLIO. What, art thou hurt?

MERCUTIO. Ay, ay, a scratch, a scratch; marry, 'tis enough. Where is my page? Go, villain, fetch a surgeon.

Exit PAGE.

ROMEO. Courage, man, the hurt cannot be much.

MERCUTIO. No, 'tis not so deep as a well, nor so wide as a church door, but 'tis enough, 'twill serve. Ask for me tomorrow, and you shall find me a grave man. I am peppered, I warrant, for this world. A plague o' both your houses! Zounds, a dog, a rat, a mouse, a cat, to scratch a man to death! A braggart, a rogue, a villain, that fights by the book of arithmetic! Why the devil came you between us? I was hurt under your arm.

ROMEO. I thought all for the best.

MERCUTIO. Help me into some house, Benvolio,
Or I shall faint. A plague o' both your houses!
They have made worms' meat of me. I have it,
And soundly too. Your houses!

Exeunt MERCUTIO *and* BENVOLIO.

ROMEO. This gentleman, the Prince's near ally,
My very friend, hath got this mortal hurt
In my behalf; my reputation stained
With Tybalt's slander—Tybalt, that an hour
Hath been my cousin. O sweet Juliet,
Thy beauty hath made me effeminate,
And in my temper softened valor's steel.

121 **aspired** ascended to.

123 **depend** hang.

124 **others** other days.

127 **lenity** gentleness.

138 **amazed** dazed.

Enter BENVOLIO.

BENVOLIO. O Romeo, Romeo, brave Mercutio is dead!
That gallant spirit hath aspired the clouds, 121
Which too untimely here did scorn the earth.

ROMEO. This day's black fate on more days doth
depend; 123
This but begins the woe others must end. 124

Enter TYBALT.

BENVOLIO. Here comes the furious Tybalt back again.

ROMEO. Alive in trumph, and Mercutio slain!
Away to heaven, respective lenity, 127
And fire-eyed fury be my conduct now!
Now, Tybalt, take the "villain" back again
That late thou gavest me, for Mercutio's soul
Is but a little way above our heads,
Staying for thine to keep him company.
Either thou, or I, or both, must go with him.

TYBALT. Thou, wretched boy, that didst consort him
here,
Shalt with him hence.

ROMEO. This shall determine that.
(*They fight.* TYBALT *falls.*)

BENVOLIO. Romeo, away, begone!
The citizens are up, and Tybalt slain.
Stand not amazed. The Prince will doom thee death 138
If thou art taken. Hence, be gone, away!

ROMEO. O, I am fortune's fool!

BENVOLIO. Why dost thou stay?
Exit ROMEO.

Enter CITIZENS.

FIRST CITIZEN. Which way ran he that killed Mercutio?
Tybalt, that murderer, which way ran he?

BENVOLIO. There lies that Tybalt.

146 **discover** uncover, reveal.

158 **nice** trivial.

168 **Retorts** returns.

172 **envious** hateful.

FIRST CITIZEN. Up, sir, go with me.
I charge thee in the Prince's name, obey.

Enter PRINCE, *attended*, MONTAGUE, CAPULET, *their* WIVES, *and all.*

PRINCE. Where are the vile beginners of this fray?

BENVOLIO. O noble prince, I can discover all
The unlucky manage of this fatal brawl.
There lies the man, slain by young Romeo,
That slew thy kinsman, brave Mercutio.

CAPULET'S WIFE. Tybalt, my cousin! O my brother's child!
O Prince! O cousin! Husband! O, blood is spilled
Of my dear kinsman! Prince, as thou art true,
For blood of ours, shed blood of Montague.
O cousin, cousin!

PRINCE. Benvolio, who began this bloody fray?

BENVOLIO. Tybalt, here slain, whom Romeo's hand did slay.
Romeo, that spoke him fair, bid him bethink
How nice the quarrel was, and urged withal
Your high displeasure. All this—utterèd
With gentle breath, calm look, knees humbly bowed—
Could not take truce with the unruly spleen
Of Tybalt deaf to peace, but that he tilts
With piercing steel at bold Mercutio's breast,
Who, all as hot, turns deadly point to point,
And, with a martial scorn, with one hand beats
Cold death aside and with the other sends
It back to Tybalt, whose dexterity
Retorts it. Romeo he cries aloud,
"Hold, friends! Friends, part!" and, swifter than his tongue
His agile arm beats down their fatal points,
And twixt them rushes; underneath whose arm
An envious thrust from Tybalt hit the life

193 **my blood** that is, the blood of my kinsman (Mercutio).

194 **amerce** punish by a fine.

201 **but murders** encourages more murders.

Of stout Mercutio, and then Tybalt fled;
But by and by comes back to Romeo,
Who had but newly entertained revenge,
And to 't they go like lightning, for, ere I
Could draw to part them, was stout Tybalt slain,
And, as he fell, did Romeo turn and fly.
This is the truth, or let Benvolio die.

CAPULET'S WIFE. He is a kinsman to the Montague.
Affection makes him false; he speaks not true.
Some twenty of them fought in this black strife,
And all those twenty could but kill one life.
I beg for justice, which thou, Prince, must give.
Romeo slew Tybalt; Romeo must not live.

PRINCE. Romeo slew him, he slew Mercutio.
Who now the price of this dear blood doth owe?

MONTAGUE. Not Romeo, Prince, he was Mercutio's
friend;
His fault concludes but what the law should end,
The life of Tybalt.

PRINCE. And for that offense
Immediately we do exile him hence.
I have an interest in your hate's proceeding,
My blood for your rude brawls doth lie a-bleeding; 193
But I'll amerce you with so strong a fine, 194
That you shall all repent the loss of mine.
I will be deaf to pleading and excuses;
Nor tears nor prayers shall purchase out abuses.
Therefore use none, Let Romeo hence in haste,
Else, when he's found, that hour is his last.
Bear hence this body and attend our will.
Mercy but murders, pardoning those that kill. 201

Exeunt.

1 **steeds** horses of Phoebus Apollo, the sun god (another name for Helios).

2 **Phoebus' lodging** the west.

3 **Phaëthon** (fā ə thon) Apollo's son, who drove the chariot of the sun too close to earth and was struck with a thunderbolt. Juliet is not aware of the ironic allusion.

SCENE 2

Juliet, awaiting Romeo's arrival, is horrified at the Nurse's news that Tybalt is dead and that Romeo has been banished. The Nurse promises to fetch Romeo, for she knows he is hidden in Friar Laurence's cell.

CAPULET'S *orchard.*

Enter JULIET.

JULIET. Gallop apace, you fiery-footed steeds, 1
Towards Phoebus' lodging! Such a wagoner 2
As Phaëthon would whip you to the west, 3
And bring in cloudy night immediately.
Spread thy close curtain, love-performing night,
That runaways' eyes may wink, and Romeo
Leap to these arms, untalked of and unseen.
Lovers can see to do their amorous rites
By their own beauties; or, if love be blind,
It best agrees with night. Come, civil night,
Thou sober-suited matron, all in black,
And learn me how to lose a winning match
Played for a pair of stainless maidenhoods,
Hood my unmanned blood bating in my cheeks
With thy black mantle, till strange love grown bold
Think true love acted simple modesty.
Come, night. Come, Romeo. Come, thou day in night;
For thou wilt lie upon the wings of night
Whiter than new snow on a raven's back.
Come, gentle night, come, loving, black-browed night,
Give me my Romeo, and when he shall die
Take him and cut him out in little stars,
And he will make the face of heaven so fine
That all the world will be in love with night
And pay no worship to the garish sun.
O, I have bought the mansion of a love
But not possessed it, and, though I am sold,
Not yet enjoyed. So tedious is this day
As is the night before some festival

37 **weraday** alas.

47 **cockatrice** the basilisk, a mythical serpent who could kill with its look.

To an impatient child that hath new robes
And may not wear them. O, here comes my nurse,

Enter NURSE, *with cords.*

And she brings news, and every tongue that speaks
But Romeo's name speaks heavenly eloquence.
Now, Nurse, what news? What hast thou there? The cords
That Romeo bid thee fetch?

NURSE. Ay, ay, the cords.
(*Throws them down.*)

JULIET. Ay me! What news? Why dost thou wring thy hands?

NURSE. Ah, weraday! He's dead, he's dead, he's dead!
We are undone, lady, we are undone!
Alack the day! he's gone, he's killed, he's dead!

JULIET. Can heaven be so envious?

NURSE. Romeo can,
Though heaven cannot. O Romeo, Romeo!
Who ever would have thought it? Romeo!

JULIET. What devil art thou that dost torment me thus?
This torture should be roared in dismal hell.
Hath Romeo slain himself? Say thou but "Ay,"
And that bare vowel "I" shall poison more
Than the death-darting eye of cockatrice.
I am not I, if there be such an "Ay,"
Or those eyes shut, that make thee answer "Ay,"
If he be slain, say "Ay," or if not, "No."
Brief sounds determine of my weal or woe.

NURSE. I saw the wound. I saw it with mine eyes—
God save the mark!—here on his manly breast.
A piteous corpse, a bloody piteous corpse;
Pale, pale as ashes, all bedaubed in blood,
All in gore-blood. I swoonéd at the sight.

JULIET. O, break, my heart! Poor bankrupt, break at once!

59 **Vile earth** that is, my body; **resign** return.

60 **bier** frame on which a corpse or coffin is carried.

67 **trumpet** the last triumpet; **general doom** Judgment Day, announced by the last trumpet.

73 **flowering** fair, like that of the serpent in the Garden of Eden.

81 **bower** give shelter to.

88 **aqua vitae** alcoholic drink.

To prison, eyes, ne'er look on liberty!
Vile earth, to earth resign, end motion here, 59
And thou and Romeo press one heavy bier! 60

NURSE. O Tybalt, Tybalt, the best friend I had!
O courteous Tybalt! Honest gentleman!
That ever I should live to see thee dead!

JULIET. What storm is this that blows so contrary?
Is Romeo slaughtered, and is Tybalt dead?
My dearest cousin, and my dearer lord?
Then, dreadful trumpet, sound the general doom! 67
For who is living, if those two are gone?

NURSE. Tybalt is gone, and Romeo banishèd;
Romeo that killed him, he is banishèd.

JULIET. O God! Did Romeo's hand shed Tybalt's blood?

NURSE. It did, it did. Alas the day, it did!

JULIET. O serpent heart, hid with a flowering face! 73
Did ever dragon keep so fair a cave?
Beautiful tyrant! Fiend angelical!
Dove-feathered raven! Wolvish-ravening lamb!
Despisèd substance of divinest show!
Just opposite to what thou justly seem'st,
A damnèd saint, an honorable villain!
O nature, what hadst thou to do in hell
When thou didst bower the spirit of a fiend 81
In mortal paradise of such sweet flesh?
Was ever book containing such vile matter
So fairly bound? O, that deceit should dwell
In such a gorgeous palace!

NURSE. There's no trust,
No faith, no honesty in men; all perjured,
All forsworn, all naught, all dissemblers.
Ah, where's my man? Give me some aqua vitae. 88
These griefs, these woes, these sorrows make me old.
Shame come to Romeo!

109 **fain** gladly.

120 **modern** ordinary.

JULIET. Blistered be thy tongue
For such a wish! He was not born to shame.
Upon his brow shame is ashamed to sit,
For 'tis a throne where honor may be crowned
Sole monarch of the universal earth.
O, what a beast was I to chide at him!

NURSE. Will you speak well of him that killed your cousin?

JULIET. Shall I speak ill of him that is my husband?
Ah, poor my lord, what tongue shall smooth thy name
When I, thy three-hours wife, have mangled it?
But wherefore, villain, didst thou kill my cousin?
That villain cousin would have killed my husband.
Back, foolish tears, back to your native spring!
Your tributary drops belong to woe,
Which you, mistaking, offer up to joy.
My husband lives, that Tybalt would have slain;
And Tybalt's dead, that would have slain my husband.
All this is comfort. Wherefore weep I then?
Some word there was, worser than Tybalt's death,
That murdered me. I would forget it fain,
But O, it presses to my memory,
Like damnèd guilty deeds to sinners' minds:
"Tybalt is dead, and Romeo banishèd."
That "banishèd," that one word "banishèd,"
Hath slain ten thousand Tybalts. Tybalt's death
Was woe enough, if it had ended there;
Or, if sour woe delights in fellowship
And needly will be ranked with other griefs,
Why followed not, when she said "Tybalt's dead,"
"Thy father," or "thy mother," nay, or both,
Which modern lamentation might have moved?
But with a rearward following Tybalt's death,
"Romeo is banishèd"—to speak that word
Is father, mother, Tybalt, Romeo, Juliet,
All slain, all dead. "Romeo is banishèd."

126 **sound** fathom.

139 **wot** know.

There is no end, no limit, measure, bound,
In that word's death; no words can that woe sound.
Where is my father and my mother, Nurse?

NURSE. Weeping and wailing over Tybalt's corpse.
Will you go to them? I will bring you thither.

JULIET. Wash they his wounds with tears? Mine shall
be spent,
When theirs are dry, for Romeo's banishment.
Take up those cords. Poor ropes, you are beguiled,
Both you and I, for Romeo is exiled.
He made you for a highway to my bed,
But I, a maid, die maiden-widowèd
Come, cords; come, Nurse; I'll to my wedding bed;
And death, not Romeo, take my maidenhead!

NURSE. Hie to your chamber. I'll find Romeo
To comfort you. I wot well where he is.
Hark ye, your Romeo will be here at night.
I'll to him. He is hid at Laurence' cell.

JULIET. O, find him! Give this ring to my true knight,
And bid him come to take his last farewell.

Exeunt separately.

SCENE 3

The Friar arrives at his cell to tell the hidden Romeo of Prince Escalus's judgment. He tries to console Romeo, telling him that though he is banished, he is after all still alive. Romeo refuses to be comforted and wishes for death. The Nurse arrives to tell Romeo of Juliet's anguish. The Friar then sends Romeo to Juliet's chamber but tells him to leave for Mantua before dawn. He proposes that Romeo stay in Mantua until the marriage is discovered and Romeo can beg for a pardon from the Prince. Romeo leaves joyfully.

1 **fearful** full of fear.

8 **doom** judgment.

10 **vanished** issued.

17 **without** outside.

FRIAR LAURENCE'S *cell.*

Enter FRIAR LAURENCE.

FRIAR LAURENCE. Romeo, come forth; come forth, thou fearful man.
Affliction is enamored of thy parts,
And thou art wedded to calamity.

Enter ROMEO.

ROMEO. Father, what news? What is the Prince's doom?
What sorrow craves acquaintance at my hand
That I yet know not?

FRIAR LAURENCE. Too familiar
Is my dear son with such sour company.
I bring thee tidings of the Prince's doom.

ROMEO. What less than doomsday is the Prince's doom?

FRIAR LAURENCE. A gentler judgment vanished from his lips;
Not body's death, but body's banishment.

ROMEO. Ha, banishment! Be merciful, say "death";
For exile hath more terror in his look,
Much more than death. Do not say "banishment."

FRIAR LAURENCE. Here from Verona art thou banishèd.
Be patient, for the world is broad and wide.

ROMEO. There is no world without Verona walls
But purgatory, torture, hell itself.
Hence "banishèd" is banished from the world,
And world's exile is death. Then "banishèd,"
Is death mistermed. Calling death "banishèd,"
Thou cutt'st my head off with a golden ax,
And smilest upon the stroke that murders me.

FRIAR LAURENCE. O deadly sin! O rude unthankfulness!
Thy fault our law calls death, but the kind prince,
Taking thy part, hath rushed aside the law,

38 **vestal** maidenly.

52 **fond** foolish.

And turned that black word "death" to "banishment."
This is dear mercy, and thou seest it not.
ROMEO. 'Tis torture, and not mercy. Heaven is here,
Where Juliet lives, and every cat and dog
And little mouse, every unworthy thing,
Live here in heaven and may look on her,
But Romeo may not. More validity,
More honorable state, more courtship lives
In carrion flies than Romeo. They may seize
On the white wonder of dear Juliet's hand,
And steal immortal blessing from her lips,
Who, even in pure and vestal modesty, 38
Still blush, as thinking their own kisses sin;
But Romeo may not; he is banishèd.
Flies may do this, but I from this must fly.
They are free men, but I am banishèd.
And sayest thou yet that exile is not death?
Hadst thou no poison mixed, no sharp-ground knife,
No sudden mean of death, though ne'er so mean,
But "banishèd" to kill me? "Banishèd"?
O Friar, the damnèd use that word in hell;
Howling attends it. How hast thou the heart,
Being a divine, a ghostly confessor,
A sin absolver, and my friend professed,
To mangle me with that word "banishèd"?

FRIAR LAURENCE. Thou fond mad man, hear me a little speak. 52

ROMEO. O, thou wilt speak again of banishment.

FRIAR LAURENCE. I'll give thee armor to keep off that word,
Adversity's sweet milk, philosophy,
To comfort thee, though thou art banishèd.

ROMEO. Yet "banishèd"? Hang up philosophy!
Unless philosophy can make a Juliet,
Displant a town, reverse a prince's doom,
It helps not, it prevails not. Talk no more.

63 **dispute** reason; **estate** state of your affairs.

77 **simpleness** foolishness.

FRIAR LAURENCE. O, then I see that madmen have no ears.

ROMEO. How should they, when that wise men have no eyes?

FRIAR LAURENCE. Let me dispute with thee of thy estate. 63

ROMEO. Thou canst not speak of that thou dost not feel.
Wert thou as young as I, Juliet thy love,
An hour but married, Tybalt murderèd,
Doting like me, and like me banishèd,
Then mightst thou speak, then mightst thou tear thy hair,
And fall upon the ground, as I do now,
Taking the measure of an unmade grave.
(*Knocking within.*)

FRIAR LAURENCE. Arise. One knocks. Good Romeo, hide thyself.

ROMEO. Not I, unless the breath of the heartsick groans
Mistlike infold me from the search of eyes. (*Knocking.*)

FRIAR LAURENCE. Hark, how they knock!—Who's there?—Romeo arise.
Thou wilt be taken.—Stay awhile!—Stand up.
(*Knocking.*)
Run to my study.—By and by!—God's will,
What simpleness is this!—I come, I come! (*Knocking.*) 77
Who knocks so hard? Whence come you? What's your will?

NURSE. (*within*) Let me come in, and you shall know my errand.
I come from Lady Juliet.

FRIAR LAURENCE. Welcome, then.

Enter NURSE.

84 **even** exactly; **case** situation.

90 **an O** a fit of groaning.

107 **sack** destroy.

NURSE. O holy Friar, O, tell me, holy Friar,
Where is my lady's lord, where's Romeo?

FRIAR LAURENCE. There on the ground, with his own tears made drunk.

NURSE. O, he is even in my mistress' case, 84
Just in her case! O woeful sympathy!
Piteous predicament! Even so lies she,
Blubbering and weeping, weeping and blubbering—
Stand up, stand up! Stand, an you be a man.
For Juliet's sake, for her sake, rise and stand!
Why should you fall into so deep an O? 90

ROMEO. Nurse! *(He rises.)*

NURSE. Ah sir! ah sir! Death's the end of all.

ROMEO. Spakest thou of Juliet? How is it with her?
Doth not she think me an old murderer,
Now I have stained the childhood of our joy
With blood removed but little from her own?
Where is she? And how doth she? And what says
My concealed lady to our canceled love?

NURSE. O, she says nothing, sir, but weeps and weeps,
And now falls on her bed, and then starts up,
And "Tybalt" calls, and then on Romeo cries,
And then down falls again.

ROMEO. As if that name,
Shot from the deadly level of a gun,
Did murder her, as that name's cursèd hand
Murdered her kinsman. O, tell me, Friar, tell me,
In what vile part of this anatomy
Doth my name lodge? Tell me, that I may sack 107
The hateful mansion. *(Drawing his sword.)*

FRIAR LAURENCE. Hold thy desperate hand.
Art thou a man? Thy form cries out thou art;
Thy tears are womanish, thy wild acts denote
The unreasonable fury of a beast.
Unseemly woman in a seeming man,

115 **tempered** balanced.

122 **wit** intellect, mind.

124 **true** proper.

127 **Digressing** if it deviates.

129 **Killing** if it kills.

143 **mishavèd** misbehaved.

146 **decreed** arranged before.

148 **watch be set** guards are posted at the city gates.

And ill-beseeming beast in seeming both!
Thou hast amazed me. By my holy order,
I thought thy disposition better tempered. 115
Hast thou slain Tybalt? Wilt thou slay thyself?
And slay thy lady, that in thy life lives,
By doing damnèd hate upon thyself?
Why railest thou on thy birth, the heaven and earth,
Since birth and heaven and earth, all three do meet
In thee at once, which thou at once wouldst lose?
Fie, fie, thou shamest thy shape, thy love, thy wit, 122
Which, like a usurer, abound'st in all,
And usest none in that true use indeed 124
Which should bedeck thy shape, thy love, thy wit.
Thy noble shape is but a form of wax,
Digressing from the valor of a man; 127
Thy dear love sworn but hollow perjury,
Killing that love which thou hast vowed to cherish; 129
Thy wit, that ornament to shape and love,
Misshapen in the conduct of them both,
Like powder in a skilless soldier's flask,
Is set a-fire by thine own ignorance,
And thou dismembered with thine own defense.
What, rouse thee, man! Thy Juliet is alive,
For whose dear sake thou wast but lately dead;
There art thou happy. Tybalt would kill thee,
But thou slewest Tybalt; there art thou happy.
The law that threatened death becomes thy friend,
And turns it to exile; there art thou happy,
A pack of blessings light upon thy back,
Happiness courts thee in her best array,
But like a mishavèd and sullen wench 143
Thou pout'st upon thy fortune and thy love.
Take heed, take heed, for such die miserable.
Go, get thee to thy love, as was decreed. 146
Ascend her chamber; hence and comfort her.
But look thou stay not till the watch be set, 148
For then thou canst not pass to Mantua,

151 **blaze** announce, proclaim.

166 **here stands all your state** your situation depends on this.

171 **hap** event.

Where thou shalt live till we can find a time
To blaze your marriage, reconcile your friends,
Beg pardon of the Prince, and call thee back
With twenty hundred thousand times more joy
Than thou wentst forth in lamentation.
Go before, Nurse. Commend me to thy lady,
And bid her hasten all the house to bed,
Which heavy sorrow makes them apt unto.
Romeo is coming.

NURSE. O Lord, I could have stayed here all the night
To hear good counsel. O, what learning is!
My lord, I'll tell my lady you will come.

ROMEO. Do so, and bid my sweet prepare to chide.

NURSE. Here, sir, a ring she bid me give you, sir.
Hie you, make haste, for it grows very late.

Exit.

ROMEO. How well my comfort is revived by this!

FRIAR LAURENCE. Go hence. Good night. And here stands all your state:
Either be gone before the watch be set,
Or by the break of day disguised from hence.
Sojourn in Mantua. I'll find out your man,
And he shall signify from time to time
Every good hap to you that chances here.
Give me thy hand. 'Tis late. Farewell, good night.

ROMEO. But that a joy past joy calls out on me,
It were a grief, so brief to part with thee.
Farewell.

Exeunt separately.

2 **move** persuade.

11 **mewed up to her heaviness** cooped up with her sorrow.

12 **tender** offer.

24 **late** lately, recently.

25 **held him carelessly** did not hold him in high regard.

SCENE 4

Capulet tells Paris that he is sure that Juliet will follow his wishes and agree to marry Paris. He sets the marriage day for Thursday.

A room in CAPULET'S *house.*

Enter CAPULET, *his* WIFE *and* PARIS.

CAPULET. Things have fall'n out, sir, so unluckily,
That we have had no time to move our daughter. 2
Look you, she loved her kinsman Tybalt dearly,
And so did I. Well, we were born to die.
'Tis very late. She'll not come down tonight.
I promise you, but for your company
I would have been abed an hour ago.

PARIS. These times of woe afford no time to woo.
Madam, good night. Commend me to your daughter.

CAPULET'S WIFE. I will, and know her mind early tomorrow;
Tonight she's mewed up to her heaviness. 11

CAPULET. Sir Paris, I will make a desperate tender 12
Of my child's love. I think she will be ruled
In all respects by me; nay more, I doubt it not.
Wife, go you to her ere you go to bed.
Acquaint her here of my son Paris' love,
And bid her, mark you me, on Wednesday next—
But soft! What day is this?

PARIS. Monday, my lord.

CAPULET. Monday! Ha, ha! Well, Wednesday is too soon;
O' Thursday let it be. O' Thursday, tell her,
She shall be married to this noble earl.
Will you be ready? Do you like this haste?
We'll keep no great ado—a friend or two;
For hark you, Tybalt being slain so late, 24
It may be thought we held him carelessly, 25
Being our kinsman, if we revel much.

32 **against** in time for.

33 **Light . . . ho** (Said to a servant.)

Therefore we'll have some half a dozen friends,
And there an end. But what say you to Thursday?

PARIS. My lord, I would that Thursday were tomorrow.

CAPULET. Well, get you gone. O' Thursday be it, then.
(*to his wife.*) Go you to Juliet ere you go to bed;
Prepare her, wife, against this wedding day. 32
Farewell, my lord.—Light to my chamber, ho!— 33
Afore me, it is so very late
That we may call it early by and by.
Good night.

Exeunt.

SCENE 5

In Juliet's chamber, Juliet and Romeo reluctantly prepare to part. The Nurse warns Juliet that her mother is approaching. Romeo and Juliet kiss and he climbs down from the window. Capulet's wife assumes that Juliet is still grieving for Tybalt and for the fact that his murderer still lives. She then informs Juliet of the wedding plans. When Capulet hears of Juliet's refusal to marry Paris, he is furious and says that he will disown her if she does not change her mind. When Juliet turns to the Nurse for help, the Nurse advises marrying Paris since Romeo is banished. Juliet is appalled and decides to seek Friar Laurence's help.

CAPULET'S *orchard.*

Enter ROMEO *and* JULIET, *above, at the window.*

JULIET. Wilt thou be gone? It is not yet near day.
It was the nightingale, and not the lark,
That pierced the fearful hollow of thine ear;
Nightly she sings on yond pomegranate tree.
Believe me, love, it was the nightingale.

ROMEO. It was the lark, the herald of the morn,
No nightingale. Look, love, what envious streaks

9 **jocund** cheerful.

13 **exhaled** Meteors were thought to be vapors drawn out of (exhaled from) the earth by the sun.

18 **so thou** if you.

20 **reflex** reflection; **Cynthia's** the moon's.

29 **division** a run of notes, once thought of as the division of a sequence of notes into several short ones.

31 **changed eyes** exchanged eyes, a reference to a folk belief.

33 **affray** frighten.

34 **hunt's-up** originally a song to awaken huntsmen, later a song to awaken newlyweds.

Do lace the severing clouds in yonder east.
Night's candles are burnt out, and jocund day 9
Stands tiptoe on the misty mountain tops.
I must be gone and live, or stay and die.

JULIET. Yond light is not daylight, I know it, I.
It is some meteor that the sun exhaled, 13
To be to thee this night a torchbearer,
And light thee on thy way to Mantua.
Therefore stay yet; thou need'st not to be gone.

ROMEO. Let me be ta'en; let me be put to death.
I am content, so thou wilt have it so. 18
I'll say yon gray is not the morning's eye,
'Tis but the pale reflex of Cynthia's brow. 20
Nor that is not the lark whose notes do beat
The vaulty heaven so high above our heads.
I have more care to stay than will to go.
Come, death, and welcome! Juliet wills it so.
How is 't, my soul? Let's talk. It is not day.

JULIET. It is, it is. Hie hence, begone, away!
It is the lark that sings so out of tune,
Straining harsh discords and unpleasing sharps.
Some say the lark makes sweet division; 29
This doth not so, for she divideth us.
Some say the lark and loathèd toad changed eyes; 31
O, now I would they had changed voices too;
Since arm from arm that voice doth us affray, 33
Hunting thee hence with hunt's-up to the day. 34
O, now begone! More light and light it grows.

ROMEO. More light and light, more dark and dark our woes!

Enter NURSE.

NURSE. Madam!

JULIET. Nurse?

NURSE. Your lady mother is coming to your chamber.
The day is broke; be wary, look about.

Exit.

43 **friend** lover.

67 **procures her hither** brings her here.

JULIET. Then, window, let day in and let life out.

ROMEO. Farewell, farewell! One kiss, and I'll descend.
(*He descends from the window.*)

JULIET. Art thou gone so? Love-lord, ay,
husband-friend! 43
I must hear from thee every day in the hour,
For in a minute there are many days.
O, by this count I shall be much in years
Ere I again behold my Romeo!

ROMEO. (*from below.*) Farewell!
I will omit no opportunity
That may convey my greetings, love, to thee.

JULIET. O, think'st thou we shall ever meet again?

ROMEO. I doubt it not; and all these woes shall serve
For sweet discourses in our time to come.

JULIET. O God, I have an ill-divining soul!
Methinks I see thee, now thou art so low,
As one dead in the bottom of a tomb.
Either my eyesight fails or thou lookest pale.

ROMEO. And trust me, love, in my eyes so do you:
Dry sorrow drinks our blood. Adieu, adieu!
Exit.

JULIET. O Fortune, Fortune! All men call thee fickle.
If thou art fickle, what dost thou with him
That is renowned for faith? Be fickle, fortune.
For then, I hope, thou wilt not keep him long,
But send him back.

Enter CAPULET'S WIFE.

WIFE. Ho, daughter, are you up?

JULIET. Who is 't that calls? It is my lady mother!
Is she not down so late, or up so early?
What unaccustomed cause procures her hither? 67

WIFE. Why, how now, Juliet!

JULIET. Madam, I am not well.

83 **like he** no man so much as he.

89 **runagate** runaway, fugitive.

90 **dram** dose.

97 **temper** mix, with double meaning of "dilute."

WIFE. Evermore weeping for your cousin's death?
What, wilt thou wash him from his grave with tears?
An if thou couldst, thou couldst not make him live;
Therefore have done. Some grief shows much of love,
But much of grief shows still some want of wit.

JULIET. Yet let me weep for such a feeling loss.

WIFE. So shall you feel the loss, but not the friend
Which you weep for.

JULIET. Feeling so the loss,
I cannot choose but ever weep the friend.

WIFE. Well, girl, thou weep'st not so much for his death
As that the villain lives which slaughtered him.

JULIET. What villain, madam?

WIFE. That same villain, Romeo.

JULIET. (*aside*) Villain and he be many miles asunder.—
God pardon him! I do, with all my heart;
And yet no man like he doth grieve my heart. 83

WIFE. That is because the traitor murderer lives.

JULIET. Ay, madam, from the reach of these my hands:
Would none but I might venge my cousin's death!

WIFE. We will have vengeance for it, fear thou not.
Then weep no more. I'll send to one in Mantua,
Where that same banished runagate doth live, 89
Shall give him such an unaccustomed dram 90
That he shall soon keep Tybalt company.
And then, I hope, thou wilt be satisfied.

JULIET. Indeed, I never shall be satisfied
With Romeo, till I behold him—dead—
Is my poor heart so for a kinsman vexed.
Madam, if you could find out but a man
To bear a poison, I would temper it, 97
That Romeo should, upon receipt thereof,
Soon sleep in quiet. O, how my heart abhors
To hear him named, and cannot come to him

101 **wreak** avenge.

112 **Marry** that is, by the Virgin Mary.

131 **bark** sailing ship.

To wreak the love I bore my cousin
Upon his body that hath slaughtered him!

WIFE. Find thou the means, and I'll find such a man.
But now I'll tell thee joyful tidings, girl.

JULIET. And joy comes well in such a needy time.
What are they, beseech your ladyship?

WIFE. Well, well, thou hast a careful father, child,
One who, to put thee from thy heaviness,
Hath sorted out a sudden day of joy
That thou expects not, nor I looked not for.

JULIET. Madam, in happy time, what day is that?

WIFE. Marry, my child, early next Thursday morn,
The gallant, young, and noble gentleman,
The County Paris, at Saint Peter's Church,
Shall happily make thee there a joyful bride.

JULIET. Now, by Saint Peter's Church, and Peter too,
He shall not make me there a joyful bride!
I wonder at this haste, that I must wed
Ere he that should be husband comes to woo.
I pray you, tell my lord and father, madam,
I will not marry yet, and when I do, I swear
It shall be Romeo, whom you know I hate,
Rather than Paris. These are news indeed!

WIFE. Here comes your father. Tell him so yourself,
And see how he will take it at your hands.

Enter CAPULET *and* NURSE.

CAPULET. When the sun sets, the earth doth drizzle dew,
But for the sunset of my brother's son
It rains downright.
How now, a conduit, girl? What, still in tears?
Evermore showering? In one little body
Thou counterfeits a bark, a sea, a wind;
For still thy eyes, which I may call the sea,
Do ebb and flow with tears; the bark thy body is,

143 **count her** consider herself.

144 **wrought** produced.

145 **bride** bridegroom.

148 **hate . . . love** that which is hateful but meant lovingly.

149 **choplogic** involved or false reasoning.

153 **fettle** make ready.

155 **hurdle** frame on which criminals were drawn to execution.

156 **greensickness** a kind of anemia in adolescent girls resulting in a yellow-green complexion; **baggage** worthless one.

Sailing in this salt flood; the winds, thy sighs,
Who, raging with thy tears, and they with them,
Without a sudden calm will overset
Thy tempest-tossèd body.—How now, wife!
Have you delivered to her our decree?

WIFE. Ay, sir, but she will none, she gives you thanks.
I would the fool were married to her grave!

CAPULET. Soft, take me with you, take me with you, wife.
How? Will she none? Doth she not give us thanks?
Is she not proud? Doth she not count her blest, 143
Unworthy as she is, that we have wrought 144
So worthy a gentleman to be her bride? 145

JULIET. Not proud you have, but thankful that you have.
Proud can I never be of what I hate,
But thankful even for hate that is meant love. 148

CAPULET. How, how, how, how, choplogic! What is this? 149
"Proud," and "I thank you," and "I thank you not,"
And yet "not proud." Mistress minion, you,
Thank me no thankings, nor proud me no prouds,
But fettle your fine joints 'gainst Thursday next 153
To go with Paris to Saint Peter's Church,
Or I will drag thee on a hurdle thither. 155
Out, you greensickness carrion! Out, you baggage! 156
You tallow-face!

WIFE. (*to* CAPULET.) Fie, fie! What, are you mad?

JULIET. Good father, I beseech you on my knees,
Hear me with patience but to speak a word.

CAPULET. Hang thee, young baggage, disobedient wretch!
I tell thee what: get thee to church o' Thursday,
Or never after look me in the face.
Speak not, reply not, do not answer me!
My fingers itch. Wife, we scarce thought us blest

168 **hilding** good-for-nothing.

171 **gossips** gossiping friends.

174 **gravity** wisdom.

177 **God's bread** the bread received in the Christian communion service.

182 **demesnes** estates.

183 **parts** qualities.

185 **puling** whining.

186 **mammet** doll; **in . . . tender** when an offer of good fortune is made.

191 **do not use** am not accustomed.

192 **advise** consider.

That God had lent us but this only child;
But now I see this one is one too much,
And that we have a curse in having her.
Out on her, hilding! 168

NURSE. God in heaven bless her!
You are to blame, my lord, to rate her so.

CAPULET. And why, my Lady Wisdom? Hold your tongue,
Good Prudence. Smatter with your gossips, go. 171

NURSE. I speak no treason.

CAPULET. O, God-i'-good-e'en!

NURSE. May not one speak?

CAPULET. Peace, you mumbling fool!
Utter your gravity o'er a gossip's bowl, 174
For here we need it not.

WIFE. You are too hot.

CAPULET. God's bread! It makes me mad: 177
Day, night, hour, tide, time, work, play,
Alone, in company, still my care hath been
To have her matched. And having now provided
A gentleman of noble parentage,
Of fair demesnes, youthful, and nobly liened 182
Stuffed, as they say, with honorable parts, 183
Proportioned as one's thought would wish a man—
And then to have a wretched puling fool, 185
A whining mammet, in her fortune's tender, 186
To answer, "I'll not wed, I cannot love,
I am too young; I pray you, pardon me."
But, an you will not wed, I'll pardon you.
Graze where you will, you shall not house with me.
Look to 't, think on 't, I do not use to jest. 191
Thursday is near. Lay hand on heart, advise. 192
An you be mine, I'll give you to my friend;
An you be not, hang, beg, starve, die in the streets
For, by my soul, I'll ne'er acknowledge thee,

216 **challenge** claim.

223 **beshrew** cursed be.

Nor what is mine shall never do thee good.
Trust to 't, bethink you. I'll not be forsworn.
Exit.

JULIET. Is there no pity sitting in the clouds,
That sees into the bottom of my grief?
O sweet my mother, cast me not away!
Delay this marriage for a month, a week;
Or if you do not, make the bridal bed
In that dim monument where Tybalt lies.

WIFE. Talk not to me, for I'll not speak a word.
Do as thou wilt, for I have done with thee.
Exit.

JULIET. O God!—O Nurse, how shall this be prevented?
My husband is on earth, my faith in heaven.
How shall that faith return again to earth,
Unless that husband send it me from heaven
By leaving earth? Comfort me, counsel me.
Alack, alack, that heaven should practice stratagems
Upon so soft a subject as myself!
What say'st thou? Hast thou not a word of joy?
Some comfort, Nurse.

NURSE. Faith, here it is.
Romeo is banished, and all the world to nothing
That he dares ne'er come back to challenge you,
Or if he do, it needs must be by stealth.
Then, since the case so stands as now it doth,
I think it best you married with the County.
O, he's a lovely gentleman!
Romeo's a dishclout to him. An eagle, madam,
Hath not so green, so quick, so fair an eye
As Paris hath. Beshrew my very heart,
I think you are happy in this second match,
For it excels your first; or if it did not,
Your first is dead—or 'twere as good he were
As living here and you no use of him.

JULIET. Speak'st thou from thy heart?

238 **forsworn** false [to my marriage vows].

242 **bosom** innermost thoughts; **twain** separated.

NURSE. And from my soul too. Else beshrew them both.

JULIET. Amen!

NURSE. What?

JULIET. Well, thou hast comforted me marvelous much.
Go in, and tell my lady I am gone,
Having displeased my father, to Laurence' cell
To make confession and to be absolved.

NURSE. Marry, I will; and this is wisely done.

Exit.

JULIET. Ancient damnation! O most wicked fiend!
Is it more sin to wish me thus forsworn,
Or to dispraise my lord with that some tongue
Which she hath praised him with above compare
So many thousand times? Go, counselor,
Thou and my bosom henceforth shall be twain,
I'll to the Friar to know his remedy.
If all else fail, myself have power to die.

Exit.

ROMEO & JULIET

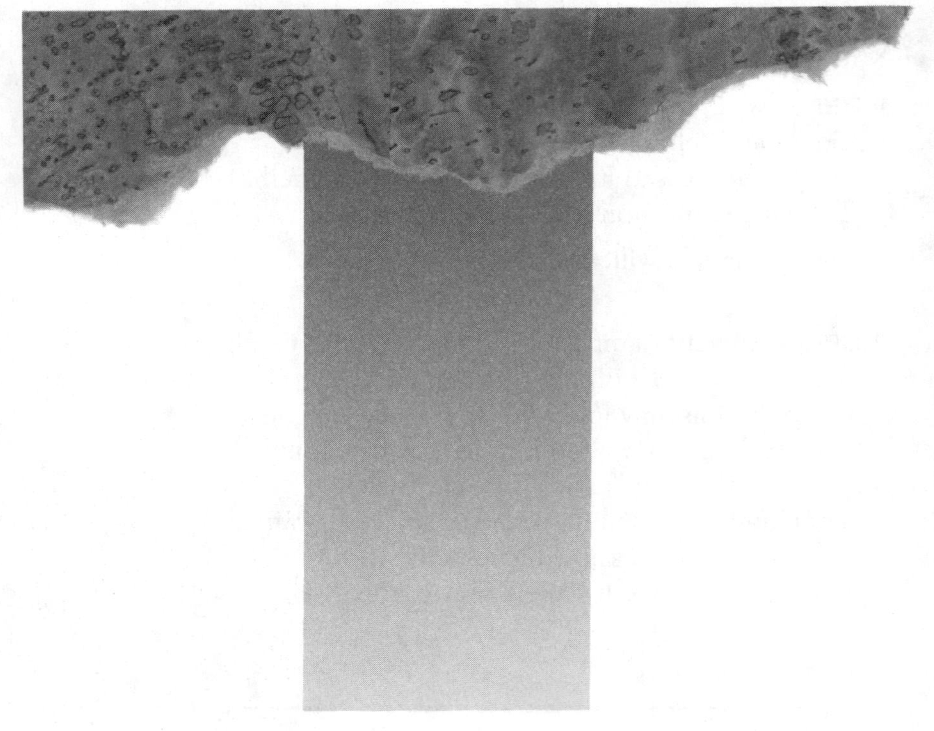

ACT IV

"Come weep with me—past hope, past cure, past help!"

2 **father Capulet** Paris is anticipating that Capulet will soon be his father-in-law.

3 **nothing . . . haste** not showing any reluctance that would make him be less hasty.

SCENE 1

Juliet enters Friar Laurence's cell while Paris is discussing his wedding to Juliet. Juliet is polite but cool and, when Paris leaves, begs the Friar for help. He gives her a potion that will simulate death and promises to send Romeo to rescue her when she awakens in the tomb. Juliet prays for strength to help her through this ordeal.

FRIAR LAURENCE'S *cell.*

Enter FRIAR LAURENCE *and* PARIS.

FRIAR LAURENCE. On Thursday, sir? The time is very short.

PARIS. My father Capulet will have it so, 2
And I am nothing slow to slack his haste. 3

FRIAR LAURENCE. You say you do not know the lady's mind?
Uneven is the course. I like it not.

PARIS. Immoderately she weeps for Tybalt's death,
And therefore have I little talked of love,
For Venus smiles not in a house of tears.
Now, sir, her father counts it dangerous
That she doth give her sorrow so much sway,
And in his wisdom hastes our marriage,
To stop the inundation of her tears,
Which, too much minded by herself alone,
May be put from her by society.
Now do you know the reason of this haste.

FRIAR LAURENCE. (*aside*) I would I knew not why it should be slowed.—
Look, sir, here comes the lady toward my cell.

Enter JULIET.

PARIS. Happily met, my lady and my wife!

JULIET. That may be, sir, when I may be a wife.

PARIS. That "may be" must be, love, on Thursday next.

JULIET. What must be shall be.

27 **price** worth.

31 **it** her face; **spite** malice.

34 **to my face** meaning both "about my face" and "openly."

40 **entreat . . . alone** ask you to leave us alone.

47 **compass** bounds.

48 **may prorogue** can delay.

FRIAR LAURENCE. That's a certain text.

PARIS. Come you to make confession to this father?

JULIET. To answer that, I should confess to you.

PARIS. Do not deny to him that you love me.

JULIET. I will confess to you that I love him.

PARIS. So will ye, I am sure, that you love me.

JULIET. If I do so, it will be of more price, 27
Being spoke behind your back, than to your face.

PARIS. Poor soul, thy face is much abused with tears.

JULIET. The tears have got small victory by that,
For it was bad enough before their spite. 31

PARIS. Thou wrong'st it more than tears with that report.

JULIET. That is no slander, sir, which is a truth;
And what I spake, I spake it to my face. 34

PARIS. Thy face is mine, and thou hast slandered it.

JULIET. It may be so, for it is not mine own.—
Are you at leisure, holy Father, now,
Or shall I come to you at evening mass?

FRIAR LAURENCE. My leisure serves me, pensive daughter, now.
My lord, we must entreat the time alone. 40

PARIS. God shield I should disturb devotion!
Juliet, on Thursday early will I rouse ye.
Till then, adieu, and keep this holy kiss.

Exit.

JULIET. O, shut the door! And when thou hast done so,
Come weep with me—past hope, past cure, past help!

FRIAR LAURENCE. Ah, Juliet, I already know thy grief;
It strains me past the compass of my wits. 47
I hear thou must, and nothing may prorogue it, 48
On Thursday next be married to this County.

54 **presently** at once.

57 **label** seal.

62 **Twixt** short for *betwixt*, between; **extremes** extreme difficulties.

64 **commission** authority.

75 **That . . . it** you, who are prepared to face death to escape the shame of marrying Paris.

81 **charnel house** place where bones of the dead are laid.

83 **reeky** reeking, smelly; **chopless** without the lower jaw.

JULIET. Tell me not, Friar, that thou hearest of this,
Unless thou tell me how I may prevent it.
If in thy wisdom thou canst give no help,
Do thou but call my resolution wise
And with this knife I'll help it presently.
God joined my heart and Romeo's, thou our hands;
And ere this hand, by thee to Romeo's sealed,
Shall be the label to another deed,
Or my true heart with treacherous revolt
Turn to another, this shall slay them both.
Therefore, out of thy long-experienced time,
Give me some present counsel, or, behold,
Twixt my extremes and me this bloody knife
Shall play the umpire, arbitrating that
Which the commission of thy years and art
Could to no issue of true honor bring.
Be not so long to speak; I long to die,
If what thou speak'st speak not of remedy.

FRIAR LAURENCE. Hold, daughter. I do spy a kind of hope,
Which craves as desperate an execution
As that is desperate which we would prevent.
If, rather than to marry County Paris,
Thou hast the strength of will to slay thyself,
Then is it likely thou wilt undertake
A thing like death to chide away this shame,
That cop'st with death himself to scape from it;
And, if thou darest, I'll give thee remedy.

JULIET. O, bid me leap, rather than marry Paris,
From off the battlements of any tower,
Or walk in thievish ways, or bid me lurk
Where serpents are; chain me with roaring bears,
Or hide me nightly in a charnel house,
O'er covered quite with dead men's rattling bones,
With reeky shanks and yellow chopless skulls;
Or bid me go into a new-made grave
And hide me with a dead man in his tomb—

94 **distilling** penetrating.

96 **humor** fluid.

97 **his native** its natural; **surcease** stop.

102 **supple government** that is, ability to move.

113 **against thou shalt awake** in anticipation of your waking.

114 **drift** plan.

119 **inconstant toy** whim.

Things that, to hear them told, have made me
tremble—
And I will do it without fear or doubt,
To live an unstained wife to my sweet love.

FRIAR LAURENCE. Hold, then. Go home, be merry, give
consent
To marry Paris. Wednesday is tomorrow;
Tomorrow night look that thou lie alone;
Let not thy nurse lie with thee in thy chamber.
Take thou this vial, being then in bed,
And this distilling liquor drink thou off, 94
When presently through all thy veins shall run
A cold and drowsy humor; for no pulse 96
Shall keep his native progress, but surcease; 97
No warmth, no breath, shall testify thou livest;
The roses in thy lips and cheeks shall fade
To wanny ashes, thy eyes' windows fall,
Like death when he shuts up the day of life;
Each part, deprived of supple government, 102
Shall, stiff and stark and cold, appear like death.
And in this borrowed likeness of shrunk death
Thou shalt continue two-and-forty hours,
And then awake as from a pleasant sleep.
Now, when the bridegroom in the morning comes
To rouse thee from thy bed, there art thou dead.
Then, as the manner of our country is,
In thy best robes uncovered on the bier
Thou shalt be borne to that same ancient vault
Where all the kindred of the Capulets lie.
In the mean time, against thou shalt awake, 113
Shall Romeo by my letters know our drift, 114
And hither shall he come; and he and I
Will watch thy waking, and that very night
Shall Romeo bear thee hence to Mantua.
And this shall free thee from this present shame,
If no inconstant toy nor womanish fear 119
Abate thy valor in the acting it.

122 **prosperous** successful.

125 **help afford** provide help.

2 **cunning** skillful.

5–6 **that cannot lick his own fingers** that is, who doesn't want to taste his own cooking.

JULIET. Give me, give me! O, tell me not of fear!

FRIAR LAURENCE. Hold, get you gone. Be strong and prosperous
In this resolve. I'll send a friar with speed
To Mantua, with my letters to thy lord.

JULIET. Love give me strength, and strength shall help afford.
Farewell, dear father!

Exeunt separately.

SCENE 2

As Capulet gives orders for wedding preparations, Juliet returns and asks for his pardon for her disobedience. Though Juliet's mother objects, Capulet now advances the wedding one day, to the next morning.

Hall in CAPULET'S *house.*

Enter CAPULET, CAPULET'S WIFE, NURSE, *and two* SERVINGMEN.

CAPULET. So many guests invite as here are writ.

Exit FIRST SERVANT.

Sirrah, go hire me twenty cunning cooks.

SECOND SERVANT. You shall have none ill, sir, for I'll try if they can lick their fingers.

CAPULET. How canst thou try them so?

SECOND SERVANT. Marry, sir, 'tis an ill cook that cannot lick his own fingers. Therefore he that cannot lick his fingers goes not with me.

CAPULET. Go, be gone.

Exit SECOND SERVANT.

10 **We . . . time** that is, we won't be ready in time.

14 **harlotry it is** hussy she is.

19 **behests** commands.

24 **tomorrow morning** Wednesday; Capulet has now moved the marriage forward a day.

26 **becomèd** befitting.

32 **bound** indebted.

33 **closet** chamber.

We shall be much unfurnished for this time. 10
What, is my daughter gone to Friar Laurence?

NURSE. Ay, forsooth.

CAPULET. Well, he may chance to do some good on her.
A peevish self-willed harlotry it is. 14

Enter JULIET.

NURSE. See where she comes from shrift with merry look.

CAPULET. How now, my headstrong! Where have you been gadding?

JULIET. Where I have learned me to repent the sin
Of disobedient opposition
To you and your behests, and am enjoined 19
By holy Laurence to fall prostrate here, (*She kneels.*)
To beg your pardon! Pardon, I beseech you!
Henceforward I am ever ruled by you.

CAPULET. Send for the County. Go tell him of this.
I'll have this knot knit up tomorrow morning. 24

JULIET. I met the youthful lord at Laurence' cell,
And gave him what becomèd love I might, 26
Not stepping o'er the bounds of modesty.

CAPULET. Why, I am glad on 't, This is well. Stand up.
(*She rises.*)
This is as 't should be. Let me see the County;
Ay, marry, go, I say, and fetch him hither.
Now, afore God, this reverend holy Friar,
All our whole city is much bound to him. 32

JULIET. Nurse, will you go with me into my closet 33
To help me sort such needful ornaments
As you think fit to furnish me tomorrow?

WIFE. No, not till Thursday. There is time enough.

CAPULET. Go, Nurse, go with her. We'll to church tomorrow.

Exeunt JULIET *and* NURSE.

44 **They are all forth** that is, the servants have all gone.

3 **orisons** prayers.

8 **behooveful** needful.

WIFE. We shall be short in our provision.
'Tis now near night.

CAPULET. Tush, I will stir about,
And all things shall be well, I warrant thee, wife.
Go thou to Juliet, help to deck up her.
I'll not to bed tonight. Let me alone.
I'll play the housewife for this once. What, ho!
They are all forth. Well, I will walk myself
To County Paris, to prepare up him
Against tomorrow. My heart is wondrous light,
Since this same wayward girl is so reclaimed.

Exeunt.

SCENE 3

Juliet dismisses her mother and the Nurse and prepares with many misgivings to drink the potion. She does so and falls upon her bed.

JULIET'S *chamber.*

Enter JULIET *and* NURSE.

JULIET. Ay, those attires are best. But, gentle Nurse,
I pray thee, leave me to myself tonight;
For I have need of many orisons
To move the heavens to smile upon my state,
Which, well thou know'st, is cross and full of sin.

Enter CAPULET'S WIFE.

WIFE. What, are you busy, ho? Need you my help?

JULIET. No, madam, we have culled such necessaries
As are behooveful for our state tomorrow.
So please you, let me now be left alone,

29 **still been tried** always been proved.

37 **conceit** idea, fantasy.

And let the Nurse this night sit up with you,
For I am sure you have your hands full all
In this so sudden business.

WIFE. Good night.
Get thee to bed and rest, for thou hast need.
Exeunt CAPULET'S WIFE *and* NURSE.

JULIET. Farewell! God knows when we shall meet again.
I have a faint cold fear thrills through my veins
That almost freezes up the heart of life.
I'll call them back again to comfort me.
Nurse!—What should she do here?
My dismal scene I needs must act alone.
Come, vial.
What if this mixture do not work at all?
Shall I be married then tomorrow morning?
No, no, this shall forbid it. Lie thou there.
(*She lays down a dagger.*)
What if it be a poison, which the Friar
Subtly hath ministered to have me dead,
Lest in this marriage he should be dishonored,
Because he married me before to Romeo?
I fear it is; and yet methinks it should not,
For he hath still been tried a holy man. 29
How if, when I am laid into the tomb,
I wake before the time that Romeo
Come to redeem me? There's a fearful point!
Shall I not then be stifled in the vault,
To whose foul mouth no healthsome air breathes in,
And there die strangled ere my Romeo comes?
Or, if I live, is it not very like,
The horrible conceit of death and night, 37
Together with the terror of the place—
As in a vault, an ancient receptacle,
Where for these many hundred years the bones
Of all my buried ancestors are packed;
Where bloody Tybalt, yet but green in earth,
Lies festering in his shroud; where, as they say,

47 **mandrakes** The root of the mandrake or mandragora plant, which was thought to resemble a person, was believed to shriek when pulled from the ground. Anyone hearing the scream was thought either to be driven mad or to die.

53 **rage** madness; **great kinsman** relation of an earlier generation, as in "great uncle."

56 **spit** impale.

2 **pastry** room where pastry is made.

At some hours in the night spirits resort—
Alack, alack, is it not like that I,
So early waking, what with loathsome smells
And shrieks like mandrakes torn out of the earth, 47
That living mortals, hearing them, run mad.
O, if I wake, shall I not be distraught,
Environèd with all these hideous fears,
And madly play with my forefathers' joints,
And pluck the mangled Tybalt from his shroud,
And in this rage with some great kinsman's bone 53
As with a club dash out my desperate brains?
O, look! Methinks I see my cousin's ghost
Seeking out Romeo, that did spit his body 56
Upon a rapier's point. Stay, Tybalt, stay!
Romeo, Romeo, Romeo! Here's drink—I drink to thee.

(*She falls upon her bed, within the curtains.*)

SCENE 4

The next morning, the Nurse, Capulet, and his wife continue their frantic wedding preparations and Capulet tells the Nurse to waken Juliet.

Hall in CAPULET'S *house.*

Enter CAPULET'S WIFE *and* NURSE.

WIFE. Hold, take these keys, and fetch more spices, Nurse.

NURSE. They call for dates and quinces in the pastry. 2

Enter CAPULET.

CAPULET. Come, stir, stir, stir! The second cock hath crowed,

5 **baked meats** pies.

6 **cotquean** man who is busy with a housewife's duties.

11 **mouse-hunt** hunter of women.

13 **jealous hood** that is, you wear the hat of a jealous person.

20 **whoreson** an abusive term, but here used in jest to mean "fellow."

The curfew bell hath rung; 'tis three o'clock.
Look to the baked meats, good Angelica.
Spare not for cost.

NURSE. Go, you cotquean, go.
Get you to bed. Faith, you'll be sick tomorrow
For this night's watching.

CAPULET. No, not a whit. What, I have watched ere now
All night for lesser cause, and ne'er been sick.

WIFE. Ay, you have been a mouse-hunt in your time;
But I will watch you from such watching now.

Exeunt CAPULET'S WIFE *and* NURSE.

CAPULET. A jealous hood, a jealous hood!

Enter three or four SERVINGMEN, *with spits and logs and baskets.*

Now, fellow, what is there?

FIRST SERVINGMAN. Things for the cook, sir, but I know not what.

CAPULET. Make haste, make haste.

Exit FIRST SERVINGMAN.

Sirrah, fetch drier logs.
Call Peter, he will show thee where they are.

SECOND SERVINGMAN. I have a head, sir, that will find out logs
And never trouble Peter for the matter.

CAPULET. Mass, and well said, A merry whoreson, ha!
Thou shalt be loggerhead.

Exit SECOND SERVINGMAN.

Good faith, 'tis day.
The County will be here with music straight,
For so he said he would. (*music within.*) I hear him near.
Nurse! Wife! What, ho! What, Nurse, I say!

Enter NURSE.

1 **Fast** fast asleep.

4 **pennyworths** small bits [of sleep].

Go waken Juliet, go and trim her up,
I'll go and chat with Paris. Hie, make haste,
Make haste. The bridegroom he is come already.
Make haste, I say.

Exeunt.

SCENE 5

When the Nurse cannot waken Juliet, she assumes that she is dead and calls forth the household. The Friar tries to comfort the grief-stricken parents and Paris. He then instructs that Juliet be entombed. The musicians, who have come to entertain the wedding guests, converse wittily with Peter.

JULIET'S *chamber.*

Enter NURSE.

NURSE. Mistress! What, mistress! Juliet! Fast, I warrant her, she. 1
Why, lamb! why, lady! Fie, you slugabed!
Why, love, I say! Madam! Sweetheart! Why, bride!
What, not a word? You take your pennyworths now. 4
Sleep for a week; for the next night, I warrant,
The County Paris hath set up his rest
That you shall rest but little. God forgive me,
Marry, and amen! How sound is she asleep!
I needs must wake her. Madam, madam, madam!
Ay, let the County take you in your bed;
He'll fright you up, i' faith. Will it not be?
(*Draws aside the bedcurtains.*)
What, dressed, and in your clothes, and down again?
I must needs wake you. Lady! lady! lady!
Alas, alas! Help, help! My lady's dead!
O, weraday, that ever I was born!
Some aqua vitae, ho! My lord! My lady!

40 **living** means of living.

Enter CAPULET'S WIFE.

WIFE. What noise is here?

NURSE. O lamentable day!

WIFE. What is the matter?

NURSE. Look, look! O heavy day!

WIFE. O me, O me! My child, my only life!
Revive, look up, or I will die with thee!
Help, help! Call help.

Enter CAPULET.

CAPULET. For shame, bring Juliet forth. Her lord is come.

NURSE. She's dead, deceased. She's dead, alack the day!

WIFE. Alack the day, she's dead, she's dead, she's dead!

CAPULET. Ha! Let me see her. Out, alas! She's cold.
Her blood is settled, and her joints are stiff;
Life and these lips have long been separated.
Death lies on her like an untimely frost
Upon the sweetest flower of all the field.

NURSE. O lamentable day!

WIFE. O woeful time!

CAPULET. Death, that hath ta'en her hence to make me wail,
Ties up my tongue and will not let me speak.

Enter FRIAR LAURENCE *and* PARIS, *with* MUSICIANS.

FRIAR LAURENCE. Come, is the bride ready to go to church?

CAPULET. Ready to go, but never to return.
O son, the night before thy wedding day
Hath death lain with thy wife. There she lies,
Flower as she was, deflowered by him.
Death is my son-in-law, Death is my heir;
My daughter he hath wedded. I will die,
And leave him all; life, living, all is Death's.

45 **lasting** unceasing.

55 **Beguiled** cheated.

61 **solemnity** festivity.

65 **Confusion's** calamity's.

66 **confusions** upheavals, disturbances.

PARIS. Have I thought long to see this morning's face,
And doth it give me such a sight as this?

WIFE. Accurst, unhappy, wretched, hateful day!
Most miserable hour that e'er time saw
In lasting labor of his pilgrimage!
But one, poor one, one poor and loving child,
But one thing to rejoice and solace in,
And cruel Death hath catched it from my sight!

NURSE. O woe! O woeful, woeful, woeful day!
Most lamentable day, most woeful day,
That ever, ever, I did yet behold!
O day! O day! O day! O hateful day!
Never was seen so black a day as this.
O woeful day, O woeful day!

PARIS. Beguiled, divorcèd, wrongèd, spited, slain!
Most detestable Death, by thee beguiled,
By cruel, cruel thee quite overthrown!
O love! O life! Not life, but love in death!

CAPULET. Despised, distressèd, hated, martyred, killed!
Uncomfortable time, why cam'st thou now
To murder, murder our solemnity?
O child! O child! My soul, and not my child!
Dead art thou! Alack, my child is dead
And with my child my joys are burièd!

FRIAR LAURENCE. Peace, ho, for shame! Confusion's
cure lives not
In these confusions. Heaven and yourself
Had part in this fair maid; now heaven hath all,
And all the better is it for the maid.
Your part in her you could not keep from death,
But heaven keeps his part in eternal life.
The most you sought was her promotion,
For 'twas your heaven she should be advanced;
And weep ye now, seeing she is advanced
Above the clouds, as high as heaven itself?
O, in this love, you love your child so ill

79 **rosemary** flower of remembrance or lasting love.

82 **fond nature** foolish human nature.

83 **nature's . . . merriment** The tears common to human nature are a time of joy to good sense or reason [because Juliet is in heaven].

85 **office** function.

90 **them** themselves.

94 **lour** look angrily.

100–101 **case . . . amended** His instrument case could be repaired or the situation could be much better, with a reference to the Nurse's "pitiful case" in line 99.

That you run mad, seeing that she is well.
She's not well married that lives married long,
But she's best married that dies married young.
Dry up your tears, and stick your rosemary 79
On this fair corpse, and, as the custom is,
In all her best array, bear her to church;
For though fond nature bids us all lament, 82
Yet nature's tears are reason's merriment. 83

CAPULET. All things that we ordainèd festival
Turn from their office to black funeral: 85
Our instruments to melancholy bells,
Our wedding cheer to a sad burial feast,
Our solemn hymns to sullen dirges change,
Our bridal flowers serve for a buried corpse,
And all things change them to the contrary. 90

FRIAR LAURENCE. Sir, go you in, and, madam, go with him;
And go, Sir Paris. Everyone prepare
To follow this fair corpse unto her grave.
The heavens do lour upon you for some ill; 94
Move them no more by crossing their high will.

Exeunt CAPULET, CAPULET'S WIFE, PARIS, *and* FRIAR.

FIRST MUSICIAN. Faith, we may put up our pipes, and be gone.

NURSE. Honest good fellows, ah, put up, put up!
For well you know this is a pitiful case.

Exit.

FIRST MUSICIAN. Ay, by my troth, the case may be amended. 100

Enter PETER.

PETER. Musicians, O, musicians, "Heart's ease, Heart's ease." O, an you will have me live, play "Heart's ease."

FIRST MUSICIAN. Why "Heart's ease"?

PETER. O, musicians, because my heart itself plays "My

107 **dump** sorrowful song or dance.

115 **gleek** jeer, jest.

116 **give you** name you.

120 **carry no crotchets** endure none of your whimsical notions, with a pun on crotchet as a musical term meaning "a quarter note."

132 **Catling** a lute string made of catgut.

135 **Rebeck** a three-stringed fiddle with a pear-shaped body.

138 **Soundpost** the peg that supports the sounding board of a musical instrument; the sounding board is a thin plate of wood.

heart is full." O, play me some merry dump to 107
comfort me.

FIRST MUSICIAN. Not a dump we! 'Tis no time to play
now.

PETER. You will not then?

FIRST MUSICIAN. No.

PETER. I will then give it you soundly.

FIRST MUSICIAN. What will you give us?

PETER. No money, on my faith, but the gleek; I will 115
give you the minstrel. 116

FIRST MUSICIAN. Then will I give you the serving-
creature.

PETER. Then will I lay the serving-creature's dagger on
your pate. I will carry no crotchets. I'll re you. I'll fa 120
you. Do you note me?

FIRST MUSICIAN. An you re us and fa us, you note us.

SECOND MUSICIAN. Pray you, put up your dagger and
put out your wit.

PETER. Then have at you with my wit! I will dry-beat
you with an iron wit, and put up my iron dagger.
Answer me like men:

"When griping grief the heart doth wound
And doleful dumps the mind oppress,
Then music with her silver sound—"

Why "silver sound"? Why "music with her silver
sound"? What say you, Simon Catling? 132

FIRST MUSICIAN. Marry, sir, because silver hath a sweet
sound.

PETER. Pretty! What say you, Hugh Rebeck? 135

SECOND MUSICIAN. I say "silver sound," because
musicians sound for silver.

PETER. Pretty too! What say you, James Soundpost? 138

THIRD MUSICIAN. Faith, I know not what to say.

142 **have . . . sounding** have no gold as payment for making music or have no gold pieces to jingle in their pocket.

147 **stay** wait for.

PETER. O, I cry you mercy, you are the singer. I will say for you. It is "music with her silver sound," because musicians have no gold for sounding:

"Then music with her silver sound,
With speedy help doth lend redress."

Exit.

FIRST MUSICIAN. What a pestilent knave is this same!

SECOND MUSICIAN. Hang him, Jack! Come, we'll in here, tarry for the mourners, and stay dinner.

Exeunt.

ROMEO & JULIET

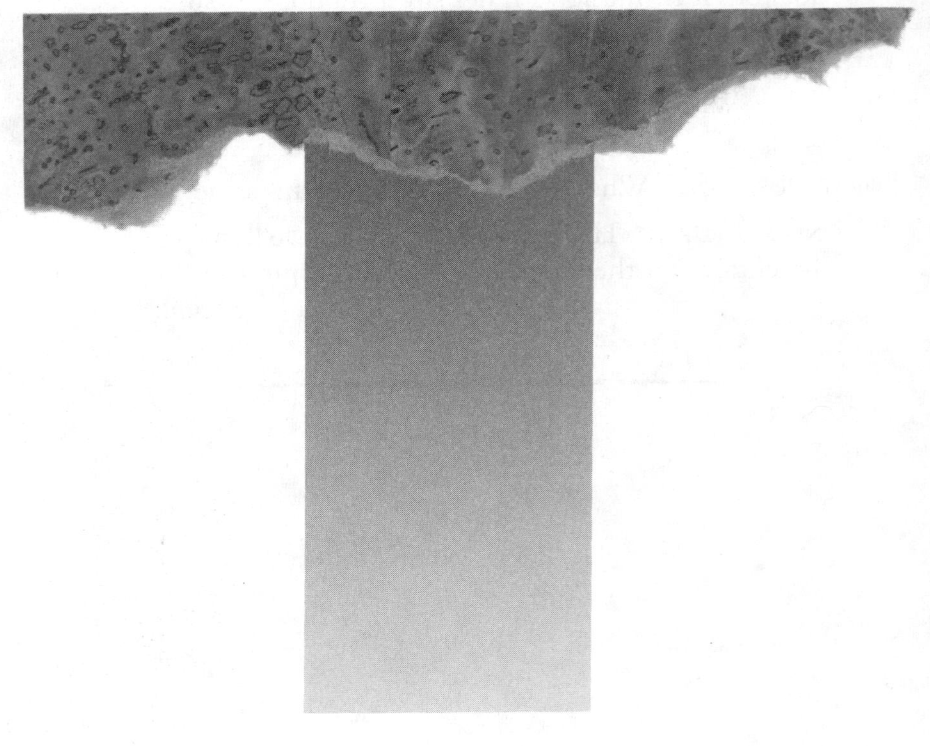

ACT V

"For never was a story of more woe
Than this of Juliet and her Romeo."

3 **bosom's lord** heart.

s.d. **booted** wearing riding boots.

21 **took post** started off with post-horses.

23 **for my office** as my duty.

SCENE 1

In Mantua, Romeo learns of Juliet's death from his servant Balthasar. He resolves to commit suicide and obtains poison from an Apothecary before starting for Verona.

MANTUA. *A street.*

Enter ROMEO.

ROMEO. If I may trust the flattering truth of sleep,
My dreams presage some joyful news at hand.
My bosom's lord sits lightly in his throne, 3
And all this day an unaccustomed spirit,
Lifts me above the ground with cheerful thoughts.
I dreamt my lady came and found me dead—
Strange dream, that gives a dead man leave to think!—
And breathed such life with kisses in my lips,
That I revived and was an emperor.
Ah me, how sweet is love itself possessed,
When but love's shadows are so rich in joy!

Enter BALTHASAR, *booted.* n

News from Verona! How now, Balthasar!
Dost thou not bring me letters from the Friar?
How doth my lady? Is my father well?
How fares my Juliet? That I ask again,
For nothing can be ill, if she be well.

BALTHASAR. Then she is well, and nothing can be ill.
Her body sleeps in Capels' monument,
And her immortal part with angels lives.
I saw her laid low in her kindred's vault,
And presently took post to tell it you. 21
O, pardon me for bringing these ill news,
Since you did leave it for my office, sir. 23

ROMEO. Is it e'en so? Then I defy you, stars!
Thou knowest my lodging. Get me ink and paper,
And hire post-horses. I will hence tonight.

37 **apothecary** druggist.

39 **weeds** clothes.

40 **simples** medicinal herbs.

47 **cakes of roses** rose petals compacted into cakes and used as perfume.

52 **caitiff** miserable.

BALTHASAR. I do beseech you, sir, have patience.
Your looks are pale and wild, and do import
Some misadventure.

ROMEO. Tush, thou art deceived.
Leave me, and do the thing I bid thee do.
Hast thou no letters to me from the Friar?

BALTHASAR. No, my good lord.

ROMEO. No matter. Get thee gone,
And hire those horses. I'll be with thee straight.
Exit BALTHASAR.
Well, Juliet, I will lie with thee tonight.
Let's see for means. O mischief, thou art swift
To enter in the thoughts of desperate men!
I do remember an apothecary, 37
And hereabouts 'a dwells, which late I noted
In tattered weeds, with overwhelming brows, 39
Culling of simples. Meager were his looks; 40
Sharp misery had worn him to the bones;
And in his needy shop a tortoise hung,
An alligator stuffed and other skins
Of ill-shaped fishes; and about his shelves
A beggarly account of empty boxes,
Green earthen pots, bladders, and musty seeds,
Remnants of packthread, and old cakes of roses, 47
Were thinly scattered to make up a show.
Noting this penury, to myself I said,
An if a man did need a poison now,
Whose sale is present death in Mantua,
Here lives a caitiff wretch would sell it him. 52
O, this same thought did but forerun my need,
And this same needy man must sell it me.
As I remember, this should be the house.
Being holiday, the beggar's shop is shut.
What, ho! Apothecary!

Enter APOTHECARY.

APOTHECARY. Who calls so loud?

59 **ducats** gold coins.

66 **mortal** deadly.

67 **utters** sells.

85 **cordial** medicine for invigorating the heart.

ROMEO. Come hither, man. I see that thou art poor.
Hold, there is forty ducats. Let me have 59
A dram of poison, such soon-speeding gear
As will disperse itself through all the veins
That the life-weary taker may fall dead,
And that the trunk may be discharged of breath
As violently as hasty powder fired
Doth hurry from the fatal cannon's womb.

APOTHECARY. Such mortal drugs I have, but Mantua's law 66
Is death to any he that utters them. 67

ROMEO. Art thou so bare and full of wretchedness,
And fearest to die? Famine is in thy cheeks,
Need and oppression starveth in thy eyes,
Contempt and beggary hangs upon thy back.
The world is not thy friend, nor the world's law;
The world affords no law to make thee rich.
Then be not poor, but break it, and take this.

APOTHECARY. My poverty but not my will consents.

ROMEO. I pay thy poverty and not thy will.

APOTHECARY. Put this in any liquid thing you will
And drink it off and if you had the strength
Of twenty men, it would dispatch you straight.

ROMEO. There is thy gold—worse poison to men's souls,
Doing more murder in this loathsome world,
Than these poor compounds that thou mayst not sell.
I sell thee poison; thou hast sold me none.
Farewell. Buy food, and get thyself in flesh.

Exit APOTHECARY.

Come, cordial and not poison, go with me 85
To Juliet's grave, for there must I use thee.

Exit.

8 **searchers of the town** officials concerned with preventing spread of plague or pestilence and with other public health matters.

18 **nice** trivial.

19 **dear** urgent.

21 **crow** crowbar.

SCENE 2

Friar John has been prevented by a quarantine from delivering Friar Laurence's instructions to Romeo. Alarmed, Friar Laurence prepares to go to the Capulet's tomb and take Juliet to his cell when she awakens, there to await Romeo.

FRIAR LAURENCE'S *cell.*

Enter FRIAR JOHN.

FRIAR JOHN. Holy Franciscan friar! Brother, ho!

Enter FRIAR LAURENCE.

FRIAR LAURENCE. This same should be the voice of
Friar John.
Welcome from Mantua. What says Romeo?
Or if his mind be writ give me his letter.

FRIAR JOHN. Going to find a barefoot brother out,
One of our order, to associate me
Here in this city visiting the sick,
And finding him, the searchers of the town, 8
Suspecting that we both were in a house
Where the infectious pestilence did reign,
Sealed up the doors and would not let us forth,
So that my speed to Mantua there was stayed.

FRIAR LAURENCE. Who bare my letter, then, to Romeo?

FRIAR JOHN. I could not send it—here it is again—
Nor get a messenger to bring it thee,
So fearful were they of infection.

FRIAR LAURENCE. Unhappy fortune! By my
brotherhood,
The letter was not nice but full of charge 18
Of dear import, and the neglecting it 19
May do much danger. Friar John, go hence.
Get me an iron crow and bring it straight 21
Unto my cell.

FRIAR JOHN. Brother, I'll go and bring it thee.

Exit.

26 **beshrew** reprove.

27 **accidents** events.

1 **aloof** apart.

FRIAR LAURENCE. Now must I to the monument alone.
Within this three hours will fair Juliet wake.
She will beshrew me much that Romeo 26
Hath had no notice of these accidents; 27
But I will write again to Mantua,
And keep her at my cell till Romeo come—
Poor living corpse, closed in a dead man's tomb!

Exit.

SCENE 3

Paris and his Page arrive at the Capulets' tomb. Warned that someone is coming, Paris hides. Romeo and Balthasar arrive, and Romeo tells Balthasar to leave him. Paris confronts Romeo and they fight. Paris is killed and Romeo opens the vault and lays Paris in the tomb. He then promises the motionless Juliet that he will never leave her, drinks the poison, and dies. Friar Laurence arrives to find the bodies of Paris and Romeo. When Juliet awakens, she sees Romeo, and in despair stabs herself. Watchmen appear and send for the Prince, the Montagues, and the Capulets. Friar Laurence recounts the story of Juliet and Romeo's marriage and the cause of her feigned death and Romeo's suicide. The Prince sorrowfully blames the enmity between the two families for this tragic event. Montague and Capulet pledge an end to their feud.

A churchyard; in it a tomb belonging to the CAPULETS.

Enter PARIS *and his* PAGE, *bearing flowers, perfumed water, and a torch.*

PARIS. Give me thy torch, boy. Hence, and stand aloof. 1
Yet put it out, for I would not be seen.
Under yond yew trees lay thee all along,
Holding thine ear close to the hollow ground.
So shall no foot upon the churchyard tread,
Being loose, unfirm, with digging up of graves,
But thou shalt hear it. Whistle then to me
As signal that thou hearest something approach.
Give me those flowers. Do as I bid thee. Go.

14 **sweet** perfumed.

15 **wanting** lacking.

16 **obsequies** funeral rites.

s.d. **mattock** pickax.

22 **wrenching iron** crowbar.

33 **jealous** suspicious.

PAGE. (*aside*) I am almost afraid to stand alone
Here in the churchyard; yet I will adventure.
(*He retires.*)

PARIS. Sweet flower, with flowers thy bridal bed I strew—
O woe! Thy canopy is dust and stones—
Which with sweet water nightly I will dew, 14
Or, wanting that, with tears distilled by moans. 15
The obsequies that I for thee will keep 16
Nightly shall be to strew thy grave and weep.
(*The* PAGE *whistles.*)
The boy gives warning something doth approach.
What cursèd foot wanders this way tonight,
To cross my obsequies and true love's rite?
What, with a torch? Muffle me, night, a while
(*He retires.*)

Enter ROMEO *and* BALTHASAR, *with a torch, a mattock, and a crowbar.* n

ROMEO. Give me that mattock and the wrenching iron. 22
Hold, take this letter. Early in the morning
See thou deliver it to my lord and father.
Give me the light. Upon thy life, I charge thee,
Whate'er thou hearest or seest, stand all aloof
And do not interrupt me in my course.
Why I descend into this bed of death
Is partly to behold my lady's face,
But chiefly to take thence from her dead finger
A precious ring, a ring that I must use
In dear employment. Therefore hence, begone.
But if thou, jealous, dost return to pry 33
In what I farther shall intend to do,
By heaven, I will tear thee joint by joint
And strew this hungry churchyard with thy limbs.
The time and my intents are savage-wild,
More fierce and more inexorable far
Than empty tigers or the roaring sea.

44 **doubt** suspect.

48 **in despite** defiantly.

68 **conjuration** warning entreaty.

BALTHASAR. I will be gone, sir, and not trouble ye.

ROMEO. So shalt thou show me friendship. Take thou that.

(He gives him money.)

Live, and be prosperous; and farewell, good fellow.

BALTHASAR. *(aside)* For all this same, I'll hide me hereabout.
His looks I fear, and his intents I doubt.

(He retires.)

ROMEO. Thou detestable maw, thou womb of death,
Gorged with the dearest morsel of the earth,
Thus I enforce thy rotten jaws to open,
And in despite I'll cram thee with more food.

(He opens the tomb.)

PARIS. This is that banished haughty Montague
That murdered my love's cousin, with which grief
It is supposèd the fair creature died,
And here is come to do some villainous shame
To the dead bodies. I will apprehend him.

(He comes forward.)

Stop thy unhallowed toil, vile Montague!
Can vengeance be pursued further than death?
Condemnèd villain, I do apprehend thee.
Obey and go with me, for thou must die.

ROMEO. I must indeed, and therefore came I hither.
Good gentle youth, tempt not a desperate man.
Fly hence and leave me. Think upon these gone;
Let them affright thee. I beseech thee, youth,
Put not another sin upon my head,
By urging me to fury. O, begone!
By heaven, I love thee better than myself.
For I come hither armed against myself.
Stay not, begone. Live, and hereafter say,
A madman's mercy bid thee run away.

PARIS. I do defy thy conjuration
And apprehend thee for a felon here.

84 **lantern** a windowed structure on top of a roof.

89 **keepers** jailers.

90 **lightening** lightening of mood.

94 **ensign** banner.

100 **his** my own.

ROMEO. Wilt thou provoke me? Then have at thee, boy!

(They fight.)

PAGE. O Lord, they fight! I will go call the watch.

Exit.

PARIS. O, I am slain! *(He falls.)* If thou be merciful,
Open the tomb, lay me with Juliet.

(He dies.)

ROMEO. In faith, I will. Let me peruse this face.
Mercutio's kinsman, noble County Paris!
What said my man, when my betossèd soul
Did not attend him as we rode? I think
He told me Paris should have married Juliet.
Said he not so? Or did I dream it so?
Or am I mad, hearing him talk of Juliet,
To think it was so? O, give me thy hand,
One writ with me in sour misfortune's book.
I'll bury thee in a triumphant grave.

(He opens the tomb.)

A grave? O, no, a lantern, slaughtered youth. 84
For here lies Juliet, and her beauty makes
This vault a feasting presence full of light.
Death, lie thou there, by a dead man interred

(Laying PARIS *in the tomb.)*

How oft when men are at the point of death
Have they been merry, which their keepers call 89
A lightening before death. O, how may I 90
Call this a lightening? O my love, my wife!
Death, that hath sucked the honey of thy breath,
Hath had no power yet upon thy beauty.
Thou art not conquered; beauty's ensign yet 94
Is crimson in thy lips and in thy cheeks,
And death's pale flag is not advancèd there.
Tybalt, liest thou there in thy bloody sheet?
O, what more favor can I do to thee
Than with that hand that cut thy youth in twain
To sunder his that was thine enemy? 100

106 **still** always.

115 **dateless bargain** everlasting contract.

Forgive me, cousin! Ah, dear Juliet,
Why art thou yet so fair? Shall I believe
That unsubstantial Death is amorous,
And that the lean abhorrèd monster keeps
Thee here in dark to be his paramour?
For fear of that, I still will stay with thee
And never from this palace of dim night
Depart again. Here, here will I remain
With worms that are thy chambermaids. O, here
Will I set up my everlasting rest
And shake the yoke of inauspicious stars
From this world-wearied flesh. Eyes, look your last!
Arms, take your last embrace! And, lips, O you
The doors of breath, seal with a righteous kiss
A dateless bargain to engrossing death!
(*He kisses* JULIET.)
Come, bitter conduct, come, unsavory guide,
Thou desperate pilot, now at once run on
The dashing rocks thy seasick weary bark!
Here's to my love! (*He drinks.*) O true apothecary!
Thy drugs are quick. Thus with a kiss I die.
(*He dies.*)

Enter, at the other end of the churchyard, FRIAR LAURENCE, *with a lantern, crowbar, and spade.*

FRIAR LAURENCE. Saint Francis be my speed! How oft tonight
Have my old feet stumbled at graves! Who's there?

BALTHASAR. Here's one, a friend, and one that knows you well.

FRIAR LAURENCE. Bliss be upon you! Tell me, good my friend,
What torch is yond that vainly lends his light
To grubs and eyeless skulls? As I discern,
It burneth in the Capel's monument.

BALTHASAR. It doth so, holy sir; and there's my master,
One that you love.

136 **unthrifty** unlucky.

145 **unkind** unnatural.

148 **comfortable** comforting.

FRIAR LAURENCE. Who is it?

BALTHASAR. Romeo.

FRIAR LAURENCE. How long hath he been there?

BALTHASAR. Full half an hour.

FRIAR LAURENCE. Go with me to the vault.

BALTHASAR. I dare not, sir.
My master knows not but I am gone hence;
And fearfully did menace me with death,
If I did stay to look on his intents.

FRIAR LAURENCE. Stay, then; I'll go alone. Fear comes upon me.
O, much I fear some ill unthrifty thing. 136

BALTHASAR. As I did sleep under this yew tree here,
I dreamt my master and another fought,
And that my master slew him.

FRIAR LAURENCE. (*advancing.*) Romeo!
Alack, alack, what blood is this which stains
The stony entrance of this sepulcher?
What mean these masterless and gory swords
To lie discolored by this place of peace?
(*He enters the tomb.*)
Romeo! O, pale! Who else? What, Paris too?
And steeped in blood? Ah, what an unkind hour 145
Is guilty of this lamentable chance!
The lady stirs.
(JULIET *wakes.*)

JULIET. O comfortable Friar! Where is my lord? 148
I do remember well where I should be,
And there I am. Where is my Romeo?
(*Noise within.*)

FRIAR LAURENCE. I hear some noise. Lady, come from that nest
Of death, contagion, and unnatural sleep.
A greater power than we can contradict
Hath thwarted our intents. Come, come away.

162 **timeless** untimely.

163 **churl** miser (she is addressing Romeo).

165 **Haply** perhaps.

173 **attach** arrest.

181 **We . . . descry** We cannot find the truth without more details.

Thy husband in thy bosom there lies dead,
And Paris too. Come, I'll dispose of thee
Among a sisterhood of holy nuns.
Stay not to question, for the watch is coming.
Come on, go, good Juliet. I dare no longer stay.

JULIET. Go, get thee hence, for I will not away.

Exit FRIAR LAURENCE.

What's here? A cup, closed in my true love's hand?
Poison, I see, hath been his timeless end. 162
O churl, drunk all, and left no friendly drop 163
To help me after? I will kiss thy lips;
Haply some poison yet doth hang on them, 165
To make me die with a restorative. (*Kisses him.*)
Thy lips are warm.

FIRST WATCHMAN. (*within.*) Lead, boy. Which way?

JULIET. Yea, noise? Then I'll be brief. O happy dagger!

(*Snatching* ROMEO'S *dagger.*)

This is thy sheath. There rust, and let me die.

(*She stabs herself and dies.*)

Enter the WATCHMAN *and* PARIS'S PAGE.

PAGE. This is the place. There, where the torch doth burn.

FIRST WATCHMAN. The ground is bloody. Search about the churchyard.
Go, some of you, who'er you find attach. 173

Exeunt some.

Pitiful sight! Here lies the County slain.
And Juliet bleeding, warm, and newly dead,
Who here hath lain these two days burièd.
Go, tell the Prince. Run to the Capulets.
Raise up the Montagues. Some others search.

Exeunt others.

We see the ground whereon these woes do lie,
But the true ground of all these piteous woes
We cannot without circumstance descry. 181

Notes

Enter some of the WATCHMEN, *with* BALTHASAR.

SECOND WATCHMAN. Here's Romeo's man. We found him in the churchyard.

FIRST WATCHMAN. Hold him in safety till the Prince come hither.

Enter FRIAR LAURENCE, *and another* WATCHMAN.

THIRD WATCHMAN. Here is a friar, that trembles, sighs, and weeps.
We took this mattock and this spade from him
As he was coming from this churchyard's side.

FIRST WATCHMAN. A great suspicion. Stay the Friar too.

Enter the PRINCE *and* ATTENDANTS.

PRINCE. What misadventure is so early up,
That calls our person from our morning rest?

Enter CAPULET, CAPULET'S WIFE, *and others*.

CAPULET. What should it be that they so shriek abroad?

WIFE. O, the people in the street cry "Romeo,"
Some "Juliet," and some "Paris," and all run
With open outcry toward our monument.

PRINCE. What fear is this that startles in our ears?

FIRST WATCHMAN. Sovereign, here lies the County Paris slain.
And Romeo dead, and Juliet, dead before,
Warm and new killed.

PRINCE. Search, seek, and know how this foul murder comes.

FIRST WATCHMAN. Here is a friar, and slaughtered Romeo's man,
With instruments upon them fit to open
These dead men's tombs.

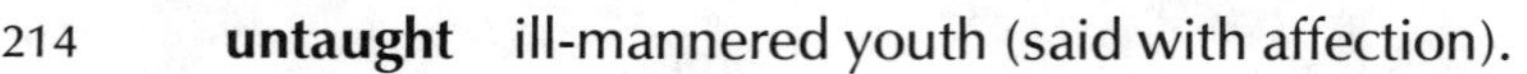

214 **untaught** ill-mannered youth (said with affection).

219 **general of your woes** the leader of your lamentation or grieving.

229 **date of breath** duration of life allowed.

CAPULET. O heavens! O wife, look how our daughter bleeds!
This dagger hath mista'en, for, lo, his house
Is empty on the back of Montague,
And it mis-sheathèd in my daughter's bosom!

WIFE. O me! This sight of death is as a bell
That warns my old age to sepulcher.

Enter MONTAGUE *and others.*

PRINCE. Come, Montague, for thou art early up
To see thy son and heir more early down.

MONTAGUE. Alas, my liege, my wife is dead tonight;
Grief of my son's exile hath stopped her breath.
What further woe conspires against mine age?

PRINCE. Look, and thou shalt see.

MONTAGUE. O thou untaught! What manners is in this,
To press before thy father to a grave?

PRINCE. Seal up the mouth of outrage for a while,
Till we can clear these ambiguities
And know their spring, their head, their true descent;
And then will I be general of your woes
And lead you even to death. Meantime forbear,
And let mischance be slave to patience.
Bring forth the parties of suspicion.

FRIAR LAURENCE. I am the greatest, able to do least,
Yet most suspected, as the time and place
Doth make against me, of this direful murder;
And here I stand, both to impeach and purge
Myself condemnèd and myself excused.

PRINCE. Then say at once what thou dost know in this.

FRIAR LAURENCE. I will be brief, for my short date of breath
Is not so long as is a tedious tale.
Romeo, there dead, was husband to that Juliet;
And she, there dead, that Romeo's faithful wife.

247 **as this** this very.

266 **privy** aware of the secret; **aught** anything.

I married them, and their stol'n marriage day
Was Tybalt's doomsday, whose untimely death
Banished the new-made bridegroom from this city,
For whom, and not for Tybalt, Juliet pined.
You, to remove that siege of grief from her,
Betrothed and would have married her perforce
To County Paris. Then comes she to me,
And with wild looks bid me devise some means
To rid her from this second marriage,
Or in my cell there would she kill herself.
Then gave I her—so tutored by my art—
A sleeping potion, which so took effect
As I intended, for it wrought on her
The form of death. Meantime I writ to Romeo
That he should hither come as this dire night
To help to take her from her borrowed grave,
Being the time the potion's force should cease.
But he which bore my letter, Friar John,
Was stayed by accident, and yesternight
Returned my letter back. Then all alone
At the prefixèd hour of her waking
Came I to take her from her kindred's vault,
Meaning to keep her closely at my cell
Till I conveniently could send to Romeo.
But when I came, some minute ere the time
Of her awaking, here untimely lay
The noble Paris and true Romeo dead.
She wakes, and I entreated her come forth
And bear this work of heaven with patience.
But then a noise did scare me from the tomb,
And she too desperate would not go with me,
But, as it seems, did violence on herself.
All this I know, and to the marriage
Her Nurse is privy; and, if aught in this
Miscarried by my fault, let my old life
Be sacrificed some hour before his time
Unto the rigor of severest law.

280 **made** did.

295 **a brace of** two.

297 **jointure** marriage settlement.

299 **raise her statue** This may refer to an effigy on a tomb, an image of the deceased in marble or stone.

PRINCE. We still have known thee for a holy man.
Where's Romeo's man? What can he say to this?

BALTHASAR. I brought my master news of Juliet's death,
And then in post he came from Mantua
To this same place, to this same monument.
This letter he early bid me give his father,
And threatened me with death, going in the vault,
If I departed not and left him there.

PRINCE. Give me the letters. I will look on it.
Where is the County's page, that raised the watch?
Sirrah, what made your master in this place?

PAGE. He came with flowers to strew his lady's grave,
And bid me stand aloof, and so I did.
Anon comes one with light to ope the tomb,
And by and by my master drew on him,
And then I ran away to call the watch.

PRINCE. This letter doth make good the Friar's words,
Their course of love, the tidings of her death;
And here he writes that he did buy a poison
Of a poor 'pothecary, and therewithal
Came to this vault to die, and lie with Juliet.
Where be these enemies? Capulet, Montague,
See, what a scourge is laid upon your hate,
That heaven finds means to kill your joys with love.
And I, for winking at your discords too,
Have lost a brace of kinsmen. All are punished.

CAPULET. O brother Montague, give me thy hand.
This is my daughter's jointure, for no more
Can I demand.

MONTAGUE. But I can give thee more,
For I will raise her statue in pure gold,
That while Verona by that name is known
There shall no figure at such rate be set
As that of true and faithful Juliet.

CAPULET. As rich shall Romeo's by his lady's lie;
Poor sacrifices of our enmity!

Notes

PRINCE. A glooming peace this morning with it brings;
The sun, for sorrow, will not show his head.
Go hence, to have more talk of these sad things.
Some shall be pardoned and some punishéd;
For never was a story of more woe
Than this of Juliet and her Romeo.

Exeunt.

Thinking About the Play

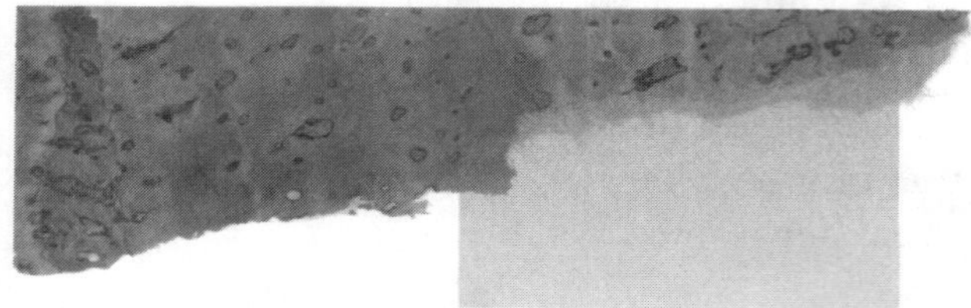

Act I

1. What are your impressions of Romeo and Juliet thus far?
2. The Prologue introduces the feud between the Montagues and the Capulets, and the characters in the play continue to bring it up. Which characters seem to take it most seriously? Which seem to want to keep the feud alive, and for what reasons? Decide if the audience should have the impression that one or two characters are most responsible for this, and find the lines the actors should stress to give that impression.
3. What does the Nurse's speech about her memories of Juliet as a baby tell you about the Nurse? For the actress playing the Nurse, list as many adjectives as you can to describe her character. You will need to convince the actress to interpret the Nurse as you see her, so list the line numbers that justify each of your adjectives.
4. What does Mercutio's speech about Queen Mab tell you about him?
5. Do Capulet and his wife seem to be good parents? Why or why not?

   Most productions play Lord and Lady Capulet as loving, even tender parents devoted to their daughter's happiness, but they can also be portrayed as unreasonable, domineering people. The real conflict will come later, but if you were directing this play, you would want to plant the seeds in the audience's mind now. Read aloud Lady Capulet's lines in Act 1, Scene 3 twice. The first time, make her seem devoted to her daughter's happiness; the second time, read her as cold and unfeeling. You might also try a third reading that places her somewhere between the two extremes.

Act II

1. After Act II, Scene 2, should the audience see Juliet or Romeo, or both, as different from what they were in Act I? Has one changed more than the other? If so, how?
2. At what points in this act is the ancient quarrel between the Montagues and Capulets recalled?
3. The Nurse calls Juliet three times in Scene 2. You can have Juliet respond calmly each time, or you can use the three interruptions in this famous scene to begin building some tension. Read aloud lines 131–155 twice, once with each interpretation. Decide which you think is more effective for the audience and explain why.
4. By the end of the act, what impression do you want the audience to have of the Nurse? What lines can best help her achieve that effect?
5. Like Juliet's parents, Friar Laurence can be played in more than one way. Many directors use him as a wise and compassionate father figure. But you can undercut some of the sentimentality of the play by instructing the actor to play the friar as somewhat slow, both physically and mentally, not always sure of what is going on or of what he is doing. Turning him into a clown would do violence to the play, though.

   Avoiding that danger, talk about both interpretations of his character (and some in between, if you like). Then decide what impression of Friar Laurence you would want to plant in the audience and how you would go about it. Consider both how the actor should read the lines and how he should manage his facial expressions and physical movements.

Act III

1. In a five-act play, Act III often contains the turning point or climax of the action. One definition of a play's climax is the point after which there is no turning back for the major character. What is the turning point in this play? Be ready to support your answer.

2. Some critics have commented that Mercutio had to be killed because he was in danger of taking over the play. What might account for this reaction to Mercutio?
3. What are Romeo's responses to news of his banishment, and how does Friar Laurence respond to Romeo?
4. Look back at your responses to question 5 for Act 1. If you've been playing Capulet as the tender father, the actor needs your help in his dramatic outburst in Scene 5. What can he do to avoid giving the audience the impression that his reaction in this scene is "out of character"? (Remember that Juliet cannot go out and get a job, nor can she go to college. When she inherits her father's estate, she will have tremendous difficulties managing it since, as a woman, she will not have the legal rights a man has. Part of a good father's responsibility is to arrange a good marriage for his daughter. Paris is handsome, rich, noble, and in love with Juliet. So since young people in the nobility often did not choose their own spouses, Capulet's choice of Paris makes substantial sense. Remember, too, that Capulet knows nothing of Juliet's love for Romeo.)
5. Discuss whether the Nurse's advice to Juliet to marry Paris is in keeping with her character. In the Franco Zeffirelli film version of *Romeo and Juliet*, the Nurse gives this advice very reluctantly. Discuss how an actress's interpretation of this advice would alter the audience's impression of the Nurse.

Act IV

1. Reread the dialogue between Juliet and Paris in Scene 1. What do her lines tell you about Juliet? If you were playing the role of Friar Laurence, how would you convey what he must be feeling during this interchange?
2. How does the Friar plan to reunite Romeo and Juliet?
3. What are Juliet's fears before she drinks the contents of the vial in Scene 3? How reasonable is each of those fears?
4. What do the speeches of those who mourn for Juliet tell you about each character?

5. If you were directing *Romeo and Juliet*, you would have to face the challenge of the musicians' scene in Scene 5 (lines 102–147). Like most modern editors, we print "Exit" at line 99 for the Nurse. But the first two printings of the play have the stage direction *Exeunt omnes*, Latin for "all exit." That would seem to signal the end of the act. Some critics have argued that it does, and that what follows was added later, possibly as a good scene for a specific actor in Shakespeare's company. Read the passage again and decide how you can use it to enhance the feeling of the scene, to relieve tension that might be building, or to provide a comment on the action of the play.

Act V

1. On the printed page, Balthasar's announcement to Romeo of Juliet's death seems unduly casual. Explain to the actor playing Balthasar how to read the lines to show that the servant cares about Romeo's feelings.
2. The information in Romeo's speech about the apothecary (Scene 1, lines 37–54) adds nothing to the plot. But what effect on the audience can it have that helps the mood of the play?
3. What are the circumstances leading to Paris's death? How many other people die during the course of the play?
4. How much responsibility does the Friar bear for the deaths of Romeo and Juliet?
5. Where does the Prince lay the blame for the tragic turn of events?

Acts I–V

1. What was your dominant impression when you finished the play? What dominant impression do you think the play should leave with an audience? Describe two or three ways you think a production can achieve that impression.
2. List the different images of light and darkness you noticed in the play. What other patterns of imagery did you find, and how could staging, lighting, music, or movement make the audience aware of them?
3. Quarrels between families, factions within a country, and nations are as common today as they were in Shakespeare's day. Is Shakespeare's message about the results of such animosities effective? Does literature have the power to alter attitudes toward bloodshed? Discuss.
4. In the seventeenth century this play was frequently given a happy ending by managers of theatrical companies anxious to please audiences. Do people prefer happy endings? Discuss.

Responding Through Writing

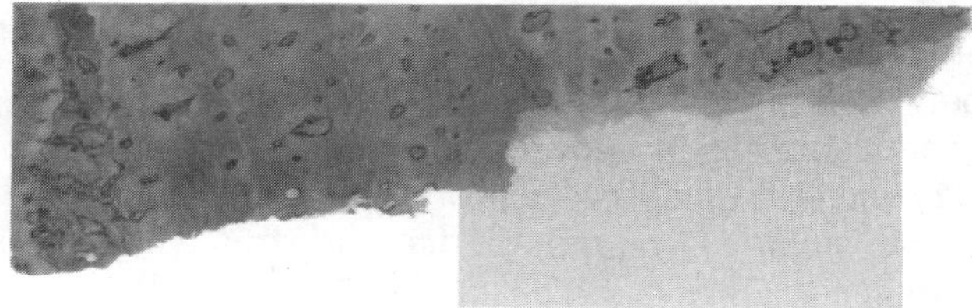

Act I

1. Juliet and Romeo are immediately attracted to each other, so much so that they kiss within minutes of meeting. How realistic is this? Is it intended to be realistic? Have Romeo's experiences with Rosaline and Juliet's knowledge that Paris wishes to marry her influenced this attraction? Examine these questions in a short paper.
2. Although Capulet has invited Paris to the feast, we are not told whether he actually appears, and he is given no lines in Scene 5. As a director, you would decide whether to put the actor playing Paris onstage. Assume for now that you want him as part of the scene. (You'll have a chance to change your mind later.) Write a note to the actor explaining why you want the audience to see Paris at the feast. Decide if you want him to enter as part of the Capulets' party or by himself. Tell him whether he should be aware of the attraction that builds so quickly between Juliet and Romeo and how he can communicate that to the audience.

Act II

1. Although Juliet and Romeo are equally passionate in their profession of love for each other, their lines reveal some differences between them. Analyze the language and content of their speeches in Scene 2 and decide what their speeches reveal.

Act III

1. Reread Juliet's famous "Gallop apace, you fiery-footed steeds" soliloquy that opens Scene 2. Make three lists: one of the allusions, one of the examples of figurative language, and one of the images. Then come to a conclusion about the overall effect the items on your lists achieve on an audience and (this will be different) on a reader.
2. For more than 300 years, critics have, as Samuel Johnson said, "frolicked in conjecturing" what the phrase "runaways' eyes" in Scene 2, line 6 might mean. You will notice that we give no note for that line, in part because we are no more sure than the scores of other editors who have wrestled with the phrase, and in part because the meaning of the sentence is clear without it. Do some detective work to find out how various critics have interpreted the phrase and come to a conclusion about the interpretation you think best fits the play.

Act IV

1. Write a character analysis of Capulet using lines from the play to support your opinions about him. Include in your analysis an explanation of the motives for his various actions. Use your notes and ideas from the questions for Acts I and III about Capulet.

Act V

1. Write two news stories about the deaths of Juliet and Romeo. Write one for a standard big-city or national daily newspaper and the other for a supermarket checkout tabloid. Stick to the facts from the play in both.
2. Write the letter that Romeo wrote to his father.

Acts I–V

1. Chance or luck plays an important part in *Romeo and Juliet*. For example, it is by chance that Romeo sees the guest list for Capulet's party. Trace the chance happenings in the play and show how each lucky or unlucky happening affects the outcome.

Enrichment Activities

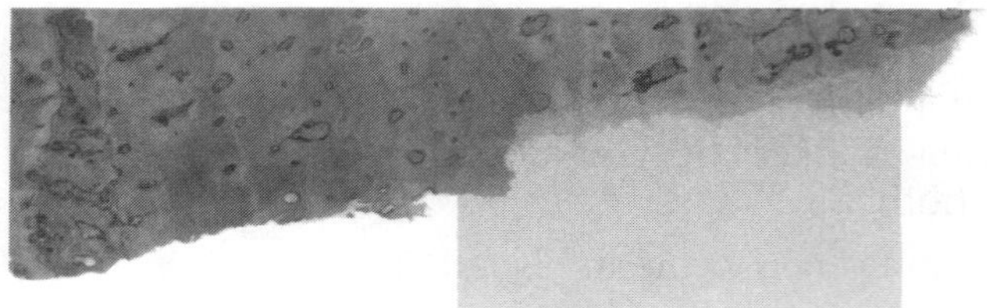

1. There are many memorable lines in this play, as proved by any book of quotations. Choose a line that appeals to you and design a greeting card, T-shirt, or poster around it. If you or someone in your class is skilled at calligraphy, you might limit your design to a few images surrounding the handwritten line.
2. With other class members, choose and perform part of a scene that has at least three characters.
3. Design a stage set for the opening scene of the play.
4. Research upper-class modes of dress during Shakespeare's time and design costumes for two or more characters to wear in the scene depicting Capulet's party.
5. Choose another appropriate setting in place and time for this play. The movie in activity 7 below uses 20th-century New York City, for instance. The Royal Shakespeare Company has played *Romeo and Juliet* in modern Verona with rival Mafia "families." What other settings might work?
6. There is a great deal of sword play in *Romeo and Juliet*. If you live in or near an area where professional or college plays are regularly produced or acting classes are given, invite an actor, drama coach, college instructor or fencing teacher to talk to the class about how actors are taught to fight onstage without hurting themselves.
7. View *West Side Story*, the film version of the stage play that was an adaptation of *Romeo and Juliet*. Write a review of the film.
8. Do research to discover what kinds of foods Capulet might have served at his feast and report to the class.

NTC SPEECH AND THEATRE BOOKS

Speech Communication

ACTIVITIES FOR EFFECTIVE COMMUNICATION, LiSacchi
THE BASICS OF SPEECH, Galvin, Cooper, & Gordon
CONTEMPORARY SPEECH, HopKins & Whitaker
CREATIVE SPEAKING, Frank
DYNAMICS OF SPEECH, Myers & Herndon
GETTING STARTED IN ORAL INTERPRETATION, Naegelin & Krikac
GETTING STARTED IN PUBLIC SPEAKING, Carlin & Payne
GETTING STARTED IN SPEECH COMMUNICATION, Lenning
LISTENING BY DOING, Galvin
LITERATURE ALIVE, Gamble & Gamble
MEETINGS: RULES & PROCEDURES, Pohl
PERSON TO PERSON, Galvin & Book
PUBLIC SPEAKING TODAY, Carlin & Payne
SELF-AWARENESS, Ratliffe & Herman
SPEAKING BY DOING, Quattrini
SPEECH: EXPLORING COMMINICATION, O'Connor

Theatre

ACTING AND DIRECTING, Grandstaff
THE BOOK OF CUTTINGS FOR ACTING & DIRECTING, Cassady
THE BOOK OF MONOLOGUES FOR ASPIRING ACTORS, Cassady
THE BOOK OF SCENES FOR ACTING PRACTICE, Cassady
THE BOOK OF SCENES FOR ASPIRING ACTORS, Cassady
DIRECTING FOR THE STAGE, Frerer
THE DYNAMICS OF ACTING, Snyder & Drumsta
GETTING STARTED IN THEATRE, Pinnell
AN INTRODUCTION TO MODERN ONE-ACT PLAYS, Cassady
AN INTRODUCTION TO THEATRE AND DRAMA, Cassady & Cassady
NTC'S DICTIONARY OF THEATRE AND DRAMA TERMS, Mobley
PLAY PRODUCTION TODAY, Mobley
STAGECRAFT, Beck

For a current catalog and information about our
complete line of language arts books, write:
National Textbook Company,
a division of *NTC Publishing Group*
4255 West Touhy Avenue
Lincolnwood (Chicago), Illinois 60646-1975 U.S.A.